Making Happiness a Habit

Making Happiness a Habit

PAUL NOWELL ELBIN

ABINGDON 🕮 festival books NASHVILLE

MAKING HAPPINESS A HABIT

A Festival Book

Copyright © 1975 by Paul Nowell Elbin

Festival edition published by Abingdon, October 1981

ISBN 0-687-23030-6 (previously published by Hawthorn Books under ISBN: 0-8015-5714-3)

HEARTFELT APPRECIATION TO

Helen, my companion and partner since high school days, whose sudden and serious illness during the writing of the last chapters of this book brought a new dimension to our love and proved for us again the paradox of happiness;

Mary Elizabeth Cox, my versatile and loyal secretary (before attainment of a Ph.D. in English literature brought her faculty status), whose scholarly work on the reference section of this book relieved me of days and days of detective work in various libraries;

Beatrice Vernet, my skillful and devoted secretary for sixteen years, for whom words are like an artist's palette and who regards manuscript typing as an act of creation.

P. N. E.

CONTENTS

Part 1

The Affirmation of Happiness

CONTENTS

Part II

The Foundations of Happiness

Part III

The Practice of Happiness

Contents

Part IV

The Unfolding of Happiness

PART I

The Affirmation
of Happiness

1

HAPPINESS CANNOT
BE GUARANTEED

A person who wants to live happily begins by recognizing the facts of life.

The most obvious fact is that life comes to us without desire or effort on our part. Life is the gift of our parents —ultimately, the religious man or woman believes, the gift of God the Creator. It is a "free" gift, without preagreed terms or conditions. Until we arrive at the age of independent decision, we cannot even reject life.

The second fact is that the gift of life carries no guarantee that life will be either easy or difficult. This is not to say that life is what we make it. There are too many formative and limiting factors to expect any life to be simply the totality of its own aspiration and effort. But a person who expects life to provide only wanted experiences assumes a provision not in the Giver's contract.

Though the ingredients of happiness are not the same for all people, all people want to be happy in their chosen way. The pursuit of happiness, Thomas Jefferson believed, is a God-given right no man may rightly deny another.

But not to deny is not to guarantee. Since the Creator allowed a very wide range of freedom for human beings, he could not create beings who would be bubblingly happy all the time. Neither God nor man can force happiness on an unwilling or foolish person.

In the ancient Hebrew book of Deuteronomy Moses describes the basic elements of human life: "I have set before you this day life and good, death and evil" (Deut. 30:15). Placing the opposites together, we face the realities: *life and death, good and evil.* These are the four basic experiences of life. Each unwritten contract for one human life guarantees all four, every one; but nothing more.

The question every person has to face eventually is this: Can I manage to find happiness in life's mixture of good and evil, life and death?

Beethoven is a marvelous example of a man who could and did. He was only twenty-eight when his hearing began to deteriorate seriously. Such an experience would be difficult enough for anyone, but for the gifted young composer-pianist it threatened the very meaning of life. His struggle was bitter, intense, lengthy. Suicide became a possibility.

After three years Beethoven had made his decision. He concluded a letter about his approaching deafness: "I will seize fate by the throat; most assuredly it shall not get me wholly down—oh, it is so beautiful to live life a thousandfold!" [1]

Thereafter in scores of musical outpourings Beethoven restated the travail of his soul, the return journey from darkness to light. Even when he could no longer hear anything he had written or anything he played, he continued to make music—the glorious music that will always identify Ludwig van Beethoven as a man who combined good and evil, life and death, in such manner as to give value and purpose to life.

For twenty-six years after his hearing began its tragic

decline, Beethoven continued to pour out the symphonies, sonatas, and concertos that will forever interpret man's spirit to man. Before his years came to an end, he had evolved a philosophy of universal significance: the belief that man must find *"joy in the struggle."*

How true it is! Moments of freedom from struggle are not common. It is a struggle to raise a family, pay the bills, keep healthy, anticipate old age, maintain decency, create beauty, live with honor. But if struggle is accepted as a normal condition of life, not as a surprising intruder, it can be handled with a joy that is distinctively human.

During a long train trip to the American Northwest some years ago, my wife and I became acquainted with a group of perhaps twenty widows who had combined loneliness to combat loneliness. Their average age was more than sixty; they had met in a Senior Citizens group.

The trip together to Seattle, Vancouver, Banff, Lake Louise, and nearby sights was from the beginning a striking example of group therapy—though from this point of view unplanned and probably unexpected. Special attention was given, but not in any sentimental manner, to the member of the group who had been widowed most recently—only a few months earlier, in fact. They agreed that "heart attacks are harder to take than cancer; they are so sudden." One told how her husband, after a day on the job, dropped his paper as he read the news following supper, and was gone.

The friendly laughter of the vacationing widows recalled the truth affirmed by Alfred Tennyson:

> 'Tis better to have loved and lost
> Than never to have loved at all.

No one in the group, however recently or however rudely bereaved, would have contested Tennyson's declaration.

His couplet, so often quoted lightly in puppy-love situations, reveals dignity and a sense of profound thankfulness when rightly understood.

Though the contract for one human life does not guarantee happiness, the ingredients of happiness are all around and within us. No one can or will, however, combine them for us. We do that for ourselves, or it is not done.

The contract contains no guarantee regarding *length of life*. The idea that people live "three score and ten" years, though it has biblical and (in a few nations) statistical support, means little to an individual.

The happiest people are those who accept, gratefully and cheerfully, the obvious fact that life in the flesh will end for each of us on some unknown date, just as childhood blended into adolescence, and as adolescence gave way to adulthood. We all live on borrowed time, no one more than another.

Man's relationship to the world of nature is in no respect more evident than in the cradle-to-the-grave nature of his existence. "We would be wise," wrote Dr. Chauncey D. Leake, "to realize that life may not be worth living when our individual genetic span has run its course." [2]

Death is a phase of life. When death comes, it should be accepted gladly as part of the entire welcome experience of living; but it should not be hurried or sought.

The implied proper behavior is indicated by reason and experience. We should be ready to die at any time. Death is the final stage of a journey which may be short or long but which should be happy in the fullest human sense.

Few people decline to accept a contract for a human life because no guarantee of happiness or long life is offered. On the contrary, most people thankfully hold on to life as long as they can. When Walt Whitman cried to his Creator, "Old, poor and paralyzed, I thank Thee," he spoke for all men.

Thomas Curtis Clark said it this way:

When I am old, and days crawl limp and slow,
When I am free from toil and weariness,
Then I shall calmly sit till sunset glow
Recounting all the hours God sent to bless.
Ten thousand dawns come again to me
To loose me from the fear of shrouding night;
Old-fashioned gardens limned by memory
Shall haunt my noontide with their pure delight.
Soft, through the windows, tender words shall come,
Voices I knew when life was April-sweet;
Then I shall sing, no more shall I be dumb;
Youth shall return, to make my joy complete.
When I am old, and quieted all strife,
My heart shall say, How good, how kind, was life! [3]

2

ATTITUDES DETERMINE
EVERYTHING

Yes, attitudes really determine almost everything. No one who has studied human nature or human physiology has failed to be impressed by the direct relationship between our attitudes and what we are in mind, body, and spirit.

Here is a famous statement of positive attitudes: "Whatever is true, whatever is honorable, whatever is just, whatever is pure, whatever is lovely, whatever is gracious, if there is any excellence, if there is anything worthy of praise, *think about these things*" (Phil. 4:8). This advice from St. Paul, from the first clause to the climactic admonition, is based upon a recognition of the importance of human attitudes.

If Paul had been a different kind of person, who believed there is small possibility of good among men, he would have phrased his counsel this way: "Whatever is false, whatever is dishonorable, whatever is unjust, whatever is impure, whatever is unlovely, whatever is cruel, if there is any deviltry, if there is any possibility of evil and misery, *think about these things*."

The person who is habitually happy is not so idealistic as not to recognize that there is a negative for every positive. To recognize that in this world there are both truth and falsehood, purity and impurity, justice and injustice is essential to mature thinking. To dwell on either the positive or the negative, to the virtual exclusion of the other, is to deny reality. Neither the Pollyanna nor the misanthrope interprets the world as it really is.

The person who thinks only dark, negative thoughts is not only unrealistic but is actually suicidal. Psychology's "death wish" is the rejection of the world. It becomes the last step in a process of unhappy thinking.

One can be sensitive to happy things, to beauty, to kindness, to what Tennyson called "the sunnier side of doubt," without neglecting or ignoring the reverse. To do so becomes, in fact, a moral and physical imperative when one contemplates the penalties of chronic unhappiness. The person who looks upon the world and sees only what is *not* good, *not* true, *not* beautiful, dies a little with each look. The furrowed brow, the scowl, the worried shake of the head, will be followed by indigestion, slackening step, breaks with folks who smile and laugh, ultimate isolation and misery.

> One child sees sunlit air and sky
> And bursting leaf buds round and ruddy;
> Another looks at his own feet
> And only sees that it is muddy.[1]

Human sensitivity can be compared to the color sensitivity of various photographic films. The original Kodachrome film emphasized blue to the point of occasional delirium. It was exciting, but it scarcely "held the mirror up to nature." Kodachrome 25 reproduces brilliant reds, but they are in balance with other colors.

Emily Dickinson's father, like his gifted daughter, was a sensitive human film—sensitive to the beauty of the world.

According to Amherst legend, the elder Dickinson was in the town square one evening when a glorious sunset began to develop. Discovering himself to be the sole viewer of the heavenly marvel, and presuming his neighbors to be at their supper tables, he ran to the fire bell and vigorously pulled the rope. When the townspeople appeared and demanded to know the location of the fire, Dickinson pointed to the majestic panorama of color and design in the West.

Each of us has had experiences in which people differed violently with regard to the interpretation of events.

I recall, for instance, a conversation among American tourists who were leaving Paris. One traveler had found nothing good about the City of Light. He had been overcharged and shortchanged. He reported *le striptease* to be as filthy in fact as the "feelthy" postcards were only claimed to be. Place Pigalle, he moaned, was a "dirty tourist trap."

But another American saw another Paris. The stained glass in the Sainte-Chapelle, seen on a sunny day, had provided an inspiration that could never be lost. He had been thrilled by the elegance and spaciousness of the Place de la Concorde and the Champs Élysées. He had made the fifty-mile trip to Chartres as a pilgrimage to faith, beauty, and history, and he had been fully rewarded.

Two young American soldiers stationed in the Deep South returned to camp on a Monday morning with very different impressions of the nearby town where they had spent a weekend leave. According to one, the town was nothing but a hellhole of brothels and saloons; everybody there lived only to cheat and rob the GI. But to the other soldier, the same town was a friendly place where you could watch a football game, attend a community dance, go to church, and be invited to a home for Sunday dinner.

This is what healthy optimism and habitual happiness

mean. You see mainly what you look for. Consider the anonymous "Good" Samaritan in the parable of Jesus. The priest and the Levite also saw the traveler who had been robbed and beaten. But they did not really see him. They saw him only as a possible threat to their arrival, on time and in proper condition, for a service of worship. The Samaritan, sensitized to human need, with his order of priorities in good repair, was the happy traveler who not only provided first aid but long-term care. With him the positive love of God instantly took ascendancy over the negative reaction of annoyance at blood, delay, inconvenience, expense.

A person who wants to live happily will do well to explore his sensitivities. Spiritually, emotionally, intellectually, we live by the things to which we become sensitive.

If unreasonable, unnecessary fear and distrust are among these things, by constructive thinking and living we can ultimately change our attitudes.

There is the fear of people, for instance, the fear of being unwanted, unappreciated, unloved. The counter interest, as opposed to fear, is the positive move to become so interested in others, so interesting to know and to associate with, so concerned about the welfare and happiness of others, that the negative factors simply disappear.

A story about a boy who lived in the mountains relates how the youngster, after being punished by his mother, ran to the precipice below his home and shouted, "I hate you!" From the distance came an angry response, "I hate you!" Frightened, the tot ran to his mother, who proceeded to give him a lesson. "Call out 'I love you,'" she suggested.

Yes, by the lessons of experience, by the deductions of thought—by earnest desire, by sincere prayer—by all these means, we purify and elevate life. We discover eventually that sensitivities can be shaped and directed. While child-hood environment is only slightly affected by our choices, *after* childhood we determine our own environment—by what we choose to read, to study, to hear on radio, to watch on television, to discuss with other people.

Color photography can shape sensitivity to the world's beauty. The discovery of white clouds against a blue sky, morning fog deep in a valley, spring blossoms in the park, silken curls on a baby, a smile of satisfaction observed on Mother's Day—these are forms of beauty reinforced and preserved by film.

When people travel a country lane, do they see only narrow roads and untended fences? Or do they see redbud trees in bloom, happy children at play, sheep grazing in safety?

When they hear "stories" about people they know, do they hear only the sordid side of rumor and gossip? Or are they concerned about the good name of an absent friend whose home, job, future, may be the target of lies?

When people are confronted with flagrant injustice, does their sensitizing apparatus go to work? Or are they conveniently disposed to pass by "on the other side"?

When a person's kindness is repaid with indifference or hostility, he can react in the spirit of the father who advised his son: "My boy, treat everybody with politeness, even those who are rude to you. Remember that you show courtesy to others not because they are gentlemen, but because you are one."

"All real joy and power of progress," John Ruskin affirmed, "depend on finding something to reverence, and all the baseness and misery of humanity begin in a habit of disdain." [2]

"*Something to reverence*"—this is the key to the life that is free and full. For all religious people, God is the primary object and inspiration for reverence. For all Christians, God and the truth incarnated in Jesus Christ are "something to reverence."

Life has value and meaning for men and women who have "something to reverence." But when "the habit of disdain" buries a life, the fears, frustrations, and unhappiness of pessimism eventually take over.

All sorts of people in unlikely circumstances have proved that life can be beautiful. What a pity then that so many people waste the gift of life by walking mainly under clouds and by slamming doors on beauty and goodness.

Emily, coming back from her grave in Grover's Corners cemetery in Thornton Wilder's *Our Town*, begins to relive her twelfth birthday. The separation from life is too much, though, and she begs to return. "Good-by to clocks ticking . . . and Mama's sunflowers. And food and coffee. And new-ironed dresses and hot baths . . . and sleeping and waking up. Oh, earth, you're too wonderful for anybody to realize you. Do any human beings ever realize life while they live it?—every, every minute?" [3]

It is a good question.

> One midnight, deep in starlight still,
> I dreamed that I received this bill:
> (———— in account with Life):
> Five thousand breathless dawns all new;
> Five thousand flowers fresh in dew;
> Five thousand sunsets wrapped in gold;
> One million snowflakes served ice-cold;
> Five quiet friends; one baby's love;
> One white-mad sea with clouds above;
> One hundred music-haunted dreams
> Of moon-drenched roads and hurrying streams;
> Of prophesying winds, and trees;

Of silent stars and browsing bees;
One June night in a fragrant wood;
One heart that loved and understood.
I wondered when I waked at day,
How—how in God's name—I could pay! [4]

3

WE CAN BE SURE
OF SOME THINGS

"Nothing is solid," laments the unhappy pessimist, citing Darwin, Marx, Freud, Nietzsche, Camus, Sartre, and other writers whose works he interprets as denying every positive value ever held by man.

"I am not certain that I believe in the good life at all any more . . . ," declares a twenty-year-old Radcliffe junior wearily. "We are all tired of trying [at twenty!]." Then she observes: "The brightest people I know don't want to do anything any more but sit around, and talk, and smoke dope." [1]

The conclusion that nothing is dependable, nothing is really good, nothing is worth trying, always results in dropout escaping from the natural life of man. Man suffocates when he attempts to live by negatives. (And people who are brightest are not always wisest.)

Without a basic conviction that human life is worthwhile, that hope and effort toward the realization of good will are not wasteful gestures, that the Creator intends a better future for man than the sadly imperfect present—without such positive beliefs, men sink into unhappy frustration, then into apathy, and finally into death of the soul.

Those who deny hope and reliability in today's world cite the perennial absence of peace and the always-suspended hydrogen bomb as well as the potent influence of certain philosophical defeatists. They observe that elements of morality vary from country to country and from generation to generation. They report that religious faith has always fluctuated between superstition and philosophy. They consider further efforts to improve human life to be "vanity of vanities," as a pessimist of long ago also concluded. They come at last to the conclusion that we cannot be sure of anything.

But we can be absolutely sure of a number of things —essential ingredients of a complete and satisfying life!

1. We can be sure there is beauty in the world.

Awareness of beauty is one of the necessary elements in a truly human existence. Though various people respond to different forms of the beautiful, no man or woman ever wholly escapes the appeal of some kinds of beauty.

Music is one of the most common. Written expression —particularly poetry—is a universally accepted embodiment of beauty. Pictures adorn the walls of the simplest homes. Beauty of form and personality in our fellow beings is everywhere appreciated. Not least, there is the world of nature, which "never did betray the heart that loved her," [2] and which for man's delight offers sailing clouds, indigo skies, racing waves, a host of flowers, and winter loveliness, such as inspired Mary Littledale to write:

> I think that God must often walk
> Deep in the winter wood,
> For seldom have I missed Him there,
> Finding His new snow good.

On every questing twig and bough,
Sweet elm and bitter bane,
Is more than the golden coin of sun,
More than the silver rain.

The silence in the waiting aisles
Leaves ears to anthems higher
Than all the choirs in the world
Could kindle or inspire.

And, meeting there, I have no words
But walk on quietly,
Gospeled by the falling snow,
Humbled by a tree.[3]

Despite evil and ugliness, who can possibly deny that there is beauty in our world or that the unspoiled man reacts with joy and thankfulness when beauty speaks directly to his soul?

2. We can be sure there is satisfying work in the world.

"Satisfying" is the right word. Weakness or illness of mind or body is usually responsible when a grown person rejects work. Healthy brains and bodies, obviously made to function, find their fulfillment only in functioning. When function ceases, life ceases.

In *Psychology in Living* Dr. Wendell White illustrated this truth by an account of a man who reached the next world suddenly and prematurely because of an unfortunate explosion. When a pleasant attendant asked for the third time in a few hours if he could do anything for the new arrival, the man answered:

"No, no," and then suddenly, "well—yes, I believe I would like to play some golf now. Will you show me the golf course?"

"We have no golf course here."

"Oh," the man replied, and added, "what are those men at the end of my cottage doing?"

"They are just completing work on it. We weren't expecting you yet."

"I'll go over and help them."

"No," said the attendant, "they will complete it for you.'

"Well, then, I'll plant my vegetables now. I always grew some of the finest on earth."

"I know you did, but here your vegetables will be cultivated and gathered for you."

"All right," the man replied, "I'll grow flowers. I have always enjoyed doing so."

"We have a flower gardener for you."

"Why, of course, I should have realized that up here there is something else for me to do. What is it?"

"Nothing."

"I don't understand. No golf, and I'm not to do any work. If I'm not to do anything here, what's heaven for?"

"Oh, mister," said the attendant, "you're not in heaven!" [4]

The unemployed man, the person retired too soon, the man or woman waiting out a lengthy period of convalescence—all testify to the truth that useful work is a blessing, that work is one of God's greatest gifts to man and is surely not the curse of Adam or any man.

3. We can be sure there is love in the world.

The greatest test of one's faith in the goodness of life —and in the goodness of God—occurs when human love turns to the bitterness of betrayal or hatred. The resulting sweeping away of emotional props can become a flood carrying away the balance of life.

Young Anne Frank, imprisoned in an Amsterdam garret by the brutal force of prejudice, daily awaiting the final moment of terror, has become a permanent image of faith that did not crack. "It's really a wonder," she confided to her diary, "that I haven't dropped all my ideals, because they seem so absurd and so impossible to carry out. Yet I keep them, because in spite of everything I still believe that people are really good at heart." [5]

The unhappy people who have concluded that there is no sincere love in this world are terribly wrong. Regardless of whatever personal hurt has influenced them, they have misread the evidence. All about us are countless examples of lives made strong and secure because of a tested friendship, a glorious marriage, or the unexpected tribute to love by an unknown person who has been helpful even when the service involved inconvenience, sacrifice, or danger.

People need to remember that you do not sit back and wait for friendship or love. You go out and earn it. You express love, and you are loved. You demonstrate friendship, and you have a friend. Even if efforts to circulate human concern are rebuffed, you grow in spirit and are strengthened for the next exercise in kindness.

The basic truth about people is that they must experience the accepting and giving of love, or they shrivel and die in spirit. Love is as essential to spiritual and mental well-being as food is to the physical.

The love of partners in a successful marriage and the mutual love of parents and children in a happy home are the most common examples of the way this principle works.

But there are other ways for the flow of love to keep a life genuinely alive. Every dedicated teacher is a third parent to every pupil. Every good pastor, whether or not he is called Father, is indeed a father in purpose and concern for others. Every worthy physician is sustained by the human factors of need and dependence, and by his response to them.

But never think that you must first qualify as a teacher, pastor, or physician in order to share a spirit-awakening relationship of love or concern for others. In every office, factory, church, school, hospital—wherever there are people—you and I will discover those to whom we can come to matter, to whom we are in fact children of God and fellow members of the human family.

Sing with honest joy, therefore, Folliott Pierpoint's familiar hymn:

> For the love which from our birth over and around us lies,
> Lord of all, to Thee we raise, this our hymn of grateful praise.[6]

4. We can be sure there is bravery in the world.

And we can be equally sure that sooner or later we will draw upon our capability for bravery. We do not order life as we order an expensive meal, confident that we will be served neatly and pleasantly, course after course. As Robert Burns observed to the fieldmouse whose nest he had accidentally destroyed,

> The best-laid schemes o' mice an' men
> Gang aft agley,
> An' lea'e us nought but grief an' pain
> For promised joy! [7]

When disaster strikes, a man should be thankful that he was designed for testing. People, as well as airplanes and bridges, are built for stress and strain, and bravery is part of the design. St. Paul was so sure of this fact that he quoted God as giving this assurance: "My grace is sufficient for you" (2 Cor. 12:9).

The first American to orbit the earth, Col. John Glenn, experienced the hot approach of death as his space capsule re-entered the earth's atmosphere. He felt something "let go." He saw "flaming chunks go flying by the window." He concluded that the capsule's heat shield was tearing apart.

Fortunately he was mistaken, and he was able to report his experience. "This was a bad moment," he recalled. "But I knew that if that was what was really happening it would be over shortly and there was nothing I could do about it. So I kept on with what I'd been doing—trying to keep the capsule under control—and sweated it out." [8]

How familiar the experience—in principle—to countless people! *"I kept on with what I'd been doing . . . and sweated it out."* What else can a man or woman do when life is rough and every resource is needed!

Consider the ordeal of Lillian Smith, the American novelist whose outpouring of conscience spoke eloquently not only to her native South but to the entire nation. Four years before her death she was honored by the Sidney Hillman Foundation with its annual magazine award and invited to New York City to receive the award in person.

Her letter of apology for not making the trip is a special profile in courage. It began: "I am sorry not to be able to say thank you in person for this award. Unfortunately, my old enemy, cancer, has chosen to interfere with my plans." Later in the letter she reported: "I have seen too much gaiety in the cobalt waiting room, heard too much laughter, watched the working of too much courage ever to despair of the human being's strength to meet ordeal and make of it something creative and good. This private experience of cancer has given me a view of courage and a love of life that I had not seen before." [9]

Thus the Maker has endowed man with the quality of bravery. Endurance, courage, and strength are all included in the shield of resistance and conquest.

5. We can be sure there is intelligence in the world.

Many people look at the condition of mankind today and despair of the future because they doubt man's capacity to deal with his most urgent problems: war, poverty, hunger, tyranny, ignorance, crime, immorality, disease, ugliness, filth, pollution, prejudice, violence, oppression, injustice.

This is an impressive list, and the reality behind each item cannot be questioned. But intelligent men draw different conclusions.

Carl Sandburg, for instance, believed what he had a character say to an audience of young people at the end of his long novel, *Remembrance Rock:* "Man is a changer. God made him a changer. You may become the witnesses of the finest and brightest era known to mankind. You shall have music, the nations over the globe shall have music, music instead of murder. It is possible. That is my hope and prayer—for you and for the nations." [10]

This is optimism. This is happiness. This is confidence and faith.

Considering the relative youth of the human race, the marvel is really that life on the earth is as safe, as ordered, as advanced as it is. Homo sapiens is a newcomer to our planet. He began very, very humbly. Not until the comparatively recent days of the Egyptians did he know much about recording his thoughts or his doings. Tribal and feudal patterns are not yet fully outgrown.

By all the logic of history, man's past should be merely the prologue to a better future.

Some clever person has worked out a scale that encourages such a hopeful thought. Think of the Washington Monument—555 feet high. Let this height represent the age of the earth. Now imagine a penny placed on top. The thickness of the penny reflects the age of man on the earth. In imagination now place on top of the penny a thin piece of tissue paper. The thickness of the paper is the period of civilization on the earth!

When a smart individual remarked, "To the astronomer, man is an infinitesimal dot in an infinite universe," a still smarter replied, "Perhaps! but man is the astronomer."

Thinking man looks back to primitive origins, and he recognizes woeful survivals of the primitive. But he also looks ahead—hopefully, prayerfully, intelligently. Having come this far, why should man not expect the slow, gradual climb to continue?

Here, then, are five ingredients of life we can be sure of: beauty, work, love, bravery, intelligence. All these we believe and accept through experience.

But through experience we must also accept the opposites: ugliness, irresponsibility, hate, cowardice, stupidity.

Throughout our lives we are confronted with positives and negatives. Both are real. And we choose between them.

4

PAINLESS LIVING
IS NOT FOR THIS WORLD

"This is painless dentistry, all right!" said the patient in the dental chair. "Grind away! It doesn't hurt a bit." And the dentist, holding a gleaming upper denture under the light, continued with his drill to shape and polish while the patient beamed.

What a perfect dream analogy of painless living! *Me* here—unhurt, unconcerned, "couldn't care less." *Over there* —all painful experience, remote, "out of this world."

A mountaineer sat on his porch strumming a guitar while the roof of his cabin burned. "Don't you know your place is on fire?" called a passerby from the road. "Yep," came the answer. "Been prayin' fer rain ever since the fahr started."

From the beginning of conscious life on the earth, man has tried one device after another in attempts to achieve painless living. Some of these attempts, of course, are beyond criticism, for without them modern medicine and dentistry would not be possible. Surgery, for example, would be in pre-ether days. And if pain killers had not been discovered, psychiatry would be deprived of some of its most helpful drugs.

But when any person gets the idea that painless living can be realized by divorcing life from hard realities, he is headed for real trouble.

Consider, for example, those drop-outs who believe painless living is possible by means of drugs. Experimenters who jump out of windows or unknowingly commit crimes are only the better-publicized examples. Much worse, because of their greater numbers, are the hideously trapped drug addicts found everywhere.

The use of opiates to escape the real world, many deluded moderns need to learn, is not new under the sun. The "other" world may indeed be fascinating, as Samuel Taylor Coleridge in an earlier century had the unique ability to describe:

> In Xanadu did Kubla Khan
> A stately pleasure-dome decree:
> Where Alph, the sacred river, ran
> Through caverns measureless to man
> Down to a sunless sea.[1]

But earth people are not Xanadu people, and opiates taken to escape responsibility and decision-making are false friends.

Physicians have found tranquilizers useful in relieving temporarily the anxieties of patients who need help because life is too much for them, people who are unable to cope with their problems.

A tranquilizer is obviously quite different from a sedative, which aims at nothing more ambitious than calming nerves. The difference is revealed in a pharmaceutical company's advertisement for a tranquilizer. The drug is expected, said the notice prepared for physicians, "to restore the patient's emotional equilibrium and normal outlook on life."

Surely this tranquilizer is not meant for the emotionally healthy individual—such as the young college instructor who dreaded his doctoral oral examination, tried to prepare himself by taking tranquilizers, and then found himself unable to respond to his questioners.

A professional singer had about the same experience. Engaged to sing with one of the country's leading symphony orchestras, he fortified himself for the occasion with a series of tranquilizing pills—and appeared as in a dream walking, with half voice, and with little ability to follow the conductor.

The hard reality of responsibility for doctoral candidates and professional singers is basically no different from the responsibilities of us all. But we should realize that when anyone faces a new or difficult situation, his body automatically prepares in all the necessary ways.

Nerves are made to whip up on occasion. In healthy people they do their special work and get back to normal, like healthy hearts that race when they need to and then quickly return to the customary pace. The public speaker or performer of any kind who does not know he has a nervous system or a heart is likely to be a bore.

Alcohol, to a much greater extent than tranquilizers and barbiturates, has become a favorite painless-living drug. The aims of the serious drinker may be more modest than the taker of pills, but the essential purposes are the same: to prepare for an unpleasant occasion, to combat loneliness, to celebrate a victory or lament a defeat, to drown sorrow or disgrace, to forget something unpleasant such as the job, the boss, the competitor. The introvert discovers that alcohol is a way of escape from himself. When drunk he can actually feel, act, talk like the uninhibited extrovert he alternately envies and despises.

The problem is that when drugs of any kind, including

alcohol, the most familiar sedative, are used to separate a person from his problems and his responsibilities (except under the careful oversight of a conscientious physician), the difficulties are likely to be multiplied, not diminished.

Wisely used, drugs can help people over rough spots in life. But they seldom remove the causes of difficulties, and if over-used they aggravate rather than alleviate. Unwisely used, drugs establish new sets of problems and new kinds of pain.

False courage is futile. Problem-solving ultimately involves inner resources that can be developed at least partially in advance and on which wise people with wise counsel can build greater strength if problems mount.

A much-used road to painless living is neutralism, a philosophy of noninvolvement, of imperturbability—a big word for a little way of life. A taxi driver demonstrated this philosophy when he apologized to a passenger for slamming on the brakes to avoid hitting a pedestrian. "Sorry," he explained, "if you hit 'em you gotta fill out a long report."

An honest question is how far down the road to neutralism a person can go and remain an authentic human being. To be fully human is to have richness of soul, interest in the welfare of others, genuine awareness of humanity's interdependence.

Edmund Burke's warning has had deserved emphasis in recent years: "The only thing necessary for the triumph of evil is for good men to do nothing." [2] Another writer states the issue with even greater force: "The hottest places in hell are reserved for those who in time of great moral crisis maintain their neutrality."

As the urbanization of our nation progresses, as impersonalization follows, the temptation for an individual to become less human grows. Yet whenever a person is hurt or dies because others were indifferent, there is, it is heartening to note, a reassuring reaction even in the farthest corners of the land. "We are on this earth to help one another," is the frequent and comforting response.

Elbert Hubbard wrote, "God will not look you over for medals, degrees or diplomas, but for scars." [3] This is the belief not only of every religion but of every humane person whether he admits to being religious or not. At Lourdes there is said to be a motel with this sign: "Gethsemane—avec tous conforts modernes." But . if Gethsemane, its spirit and significance, is part of the soul of man, it cannot be retained "with all modern comforts."

It was not Karl Marx who first called religion the opiate of the people. It was an English clergyman, Charles Kingsley, who was so disappointed with what was passing for Christianity in his time, especially the indifference of churchmen to social injustice, that he tried to arouse the conscience of Christians by terming religion an opiate.

Kingsley and Marx would probably agree that institutionalized religion always needs to fight against the opiate tendency. On the cross, Jesus refused an opiate. A church composed of true followers of Jesus could never become a way to painless living through a philosophy of noninvolvement.

Painless living is experienced only by certain of the mentally ill, men or women who lose the battle of adjustment to an imperfect world, who finally separate self from reality, who at last retreat into an inner world. This form of functional psychosis, called insanity by the law, is as close to painless living as mortals can experience. But it is not living. It is living death.

Happy living does not mean life without pain. Life is never painless, but pain can be endured.

The ultimate purpose of science, medicine, education, and religion is not to remove the stresses and hazards of life. The main purpose is to help people face life with the habit of happiness as a dependable ally.

To live is to have problems, some of them painful. To live fully is to discover that strength comes through struggle and that peace of mind comes through conquest.

This is what the Master of all Christians meant when, facing the death of the cross, he said to his friends, "I have overcome the world" (John 16:33).

5

CELEBRATE LIFE!

"If the stars came out only once a year," a philosophic person reflected, "the whole world would go out and look at them."

If there were only one magnificent sunset a year, one friendly handshake a year, one word of appreciation a year —how special, how precious they would be!

A farmer's wife, a woman who had cooked for a large family and several farm hands for thirty years, one day served boiled cattle fodder for dinner. When her husband asked if she had gone crazy, she answered, "In thirty years I never heard anything to make me think it made any difference what I cooked."

The dull acceptance of life, even its highlights of kindness and beauty and cheer, is the chief obstacle to happiness. Open eyes, ears, brains—alert to the fascination of the universe—are prerequisites to happiness. Brooks Atkinson underscored this when he wrote, "Nothing is uninteresting; there are only uninterested people."

As my years accumulate, I understand better and better what Bernard Berenson, the eminent art critic, said when he was nearly ninety: "I would willingly stand at street corners, hat in hand, begging passers-by to drop their unused minutes in it." [1]

Call this attitude toward life what you will, it is religious in the deepest sense. The celebration of life is the adoration of God, and worship is the religious man's preventive for the dull acceptance of life.

"Let us come into his presence with thanksgiving; let us make a joyful noise to him with songs of praise! . . . let us kneel before the Lord, our Maker" (Ps. 95:2-3, 6b). Thus reads a hearty hymn sung vigorously in the temple at Jerusalem more than two millennia ago. It affirms for all people of all time the essential goodness of life.

However men worship, in public or in private, in grandeur or in simplicity, they declare this common creed: Life with its burden and pain, life with its joy and ecstasy, is worth living. Thanks to the Giver of life! With Albert Camus, men discover that "The harshest winter finds an invincible summer in us." Though Camus would not agree, this summer, for the believer, is God at work in human life.

Not all men and women, as we know, "read" God and man in this manner. A struggling campus poet, for example, sees human life like this:

> Sing a song of sadness
> And loud is the refrain
> Many come to join you
> To lift and swell the strain
> Not your fellow moaners
> In full harmony weep
> Spend a lifetime wailing—
> Till off to death you creep. [2]

Contemporary atheists are naive to think they represent a new viewpoint. To be sure, with the demise of medievalism in religion, the believers in Man-Is-All have gained new acceptance and respectability. Some forms of Humanism, Existentialism, Logical Positivism, Pragmatism, Marxism, psychoanalysis, anthropology, and sociology have been taught to groping students as the final blow to an imaginary God.

But free thinkers do not necessarily become atheists. In our generation honest searchers for truth often arrive at a spiritualized faith they discover within the religious accretion of centuries.

They are moderns who find intellectually defensible ways to celebrate life. They believe that God "created man in his own image . . . ; male and female he created them." They are not impressed when a Berkeley professor maintains that "[Man is], and seems likely to remain, a somewhat altered fish, a slightly remodeled ape." [3] Hamlet's exclamation, "What a piece of work is a man! how noble in reason! how infinite in faculty!" [4] describes their faith and hopes better than the lament of Mark Twain that "man is the poorest, clumsiest excuse of all the creatures that inhabit the earth."

Thomas Curtis Clark aptly described these two viewpoints in his poem titled "Life":

I

> Poor victims we! Through time and space
> We thread our paths, from dark to dark.
> Across the earth's dumb, joyless face
> We crawl until age retards our pace.
> Once more we view the landscape stark
> Then drop into our tomb.
> No spark
> Illumines its sepulchral gloom.

II

> God's pilgrims we! From some far shore
> We come to this bright realm of flowers.
> We pause at youth's enchanted door,
> Then take our way. Abundant store
> Of joy and dreams and flowers is ours.
> The sunset comes, then night:
> In bowers
> Of fronded ferns we wait the Light.[5]

Life, of course, is not *all* darkness or *all* light. This truism is the premise for *Making Happiness a Habit*. Some unfortunate people, though, do decide that basically life is a "dumb, joyless" experience and thereby shut out an "abundant store of joy and dreams and flowers." The well-adjusted personality accepts life's mixture of happy and unhappy experiences as a constant challenge to strength, compassion, and purpose.

Those people who seldom rise above cynicism and negation are poor companions for themselves and everyone around them. A sixteen-year-old girl who took her own life left this note addressed to her mother: "It seems I never did anything right." Possibly the sensitive teen-ager simply could not cope with the conflicting pressures of growing up. Her pitiful death note, though, suggests that two people were involved in a communication gap.

A grieving husband handed a worn volume of poems to the minister who was to conduct his wife's funeral service. "It's hers," he explained. "She liked poems—was always wanting to read them to me. It seemed I never had time to listen. I guess some people don't learn what time is for 'til it's too late."

The "dumb, joyless" outlook of some Americans, I fear,

is affecting our nation's morale without guaranteeing significant improvement in our collective life. Such Americans cynically observe the partially realized dream of our founding fathers and the patriots of twenty decades; then they condemn the land of their birth as hypocritical and imperialistic. Ignorantly, some look to the Soviet or Chinese heartlands of totalitarian Communism as models for a twentieth-century form of freedom.

Surely our country needs critics—the kinds of critics who are usually imprisoned, exiled, or killed in competing forms of society. Americanism is best demonstrated by citizens who seek to have our land conform to the ideals that are noblest and highest in our tradition. Those who are unaware of imperfections in our "liberty-and-justice-for-all" society are not really good Americans.

Most of us are painfully conscious of hateful racial prejudice; of bitterness and crime that turn cities into armed enclaves; of a growing addiction to alcohol, heroin, and other drugs by young and old; of foreign policy that appears at times to be dominated by forces unlikely to serve our nation's best interests; of wasteful exhaustion of resources and of dangerous pollution; of the rapid substitution of paganism for the Hebrew-Christian foundations of our national culture. We Americans have plenty to worry and pray about.

But these vital concerns could easily cause us to overlook the accomplishments of the diverse peoples who have assembled in our fifty states. Comments by two members of an Oxford University debate team following an American tour should help put our problems in perspective. "It does seem to us," they wrote, "that Americans have become so obsessed with their problems as to forget the fantastic achievements of their country. . . . It is the economic achievement which is the most striking. . . . The general living standards [are] incredible by

European standards—but even the poor are not that badly off. Few people here realize that a Black in the South of America stands a far better chance of going to college than any child in Britain. . . . In the field of Civil Rights, more is being done to achieve racial equality than anywhere else in the world facing the same problem."

Continuing their evaluation of the United States, the visiting English debaters observed, "Americans forget how lucky they are to be able to criticize their government so freely. The underdeveloped world is dominated by totalitarian military regimes. In the Communist world, American-style freedom is not even conceived." [6] These students could not be more right.

Jean-François Revel, looking from France at our chief social problem, makes this thoughtful statement in *Without Marx or Jesus*: "The battle for black rights since 1954 . . . has been a winning battle. Today, there are 434,-000 black students in American universities, out of a total black population of 22 million—a ratio higher than that of French university students to France's 50 million inhabitants." [7]

Those concerned Americans who feel they cannot celebrate life in America because of our social, economic, and political faults should visit, as I did not long ago, the land of Lenin. No doubt the masses there are better off economically than they were in Czarist days. But an observing, thinking visitor soon discovers ugly reality behind the pretty facade. Naive in the extreme is the American who goes to the Soviet Union and sees only clean streets, marble subway stations, wedding-cake Stalin-era buildings, and crowded universities.

Europe and Asia from the middle of Germany to the far-away Pacific Ocean constitute one gigantic Soviet prison where people are taught to read but denied access to the truth, are taught to participate in sports but not in government, are taught to create but only what the nonre-callable one-party government approves.

Far from being a deviation from the theme of this book, this challenge to find reason to celebrate life in America is relevant and needful. When I returned from Eastern Europe, I thanked God for the privilege of living in a nation that after two hundred years adheres to these essentials of freedom and dignity:

1. The right of an opposition political party to function without harassment and to return to power without violence.

2. The right of the people through established legal procedures to hold public officials accountable for their actions.

3. The right of newsgatherers to report their findings to the people without interference or censorship.

When Daniel Webster delivered the dedicatory oration for the Bunker Hill monument, an enormous crowd surged toward the platform until people were being crushed. Alarmed officers tried to get the throng to fall back, but people yelled, "Impossible!" Then Daniel Webster applied his sense of crowd psychology and his faith in his hearers' rationality. He thundered, "Impossible? *Nothing* is impossible on Bunker Hill!" The crowd relaxed, and lives were saved.

Among those of us who live in the last third of the twentieth century are some, alas, who will not celebrate life—and adore the Creator of life. A minister, God save his soul, told a Thanksgiving Sunday congregation that he would have preached a thanksgiving sermon if there were anything to be thankful for.

God has given his human family all the ingredients necessary for creating heaven on earth. But the family has fought for selfish advantage among its divisions, and sin has marred happiness through all generations.

With God as our Guide and Christ as our Savior, we can be sure that *nothing* is impossible for tomorrow and tomorrow and tomorrow.

Edgar Lee Masters, inspired by the life of his grandmother, wrote "Lucinda Matlock" as a challenge to the descendants of pioneer Americans. Read this and take heart:

I went to the dances at Chandlerville,
And played snap-out at Winchester.
One time we changed partners,
Driving home in the moonlight of middle June,
And then I found Davis.
We were married and lived together for seventy years,
Enjoying, working, raising the twelve children,
Eight of whom we lost
Ere I had reached the age of sixty.
I spun, I wove, I kept the house, I nursed the sick,
I made the garden, and for holiday
Rambled over the fields where sang the larks,
And by Spoon River gathering many a shell,
And many a flower and medicinal weed—
Shouting to the wooded hills, singing to the green valleys,
At ninety-six I had lived enough, that is all,
And passed to a sweet repose.
What is this I hear of sorrow and weariness,
Anger, discontent and drooping hopes?
Degenerate sons and daughters,
Life is too strong for you—
It takes life to love Life.[8]

PART II

The Foundations of Happiness

6

GOD IS REAL

Humility in searching for an understanding of God is a vital necessity. Loud-mouthed orators, pulpit or otherwise, who presume to know all and tell all about God are not to be trusted. Anyone who has traveled even in the borderland of Eternal Truth is a humble person. After God had spoken to Job from the storm, had asked him question after question that no man can answer, Job confessed: "Therefore I have uttered what I did not understand, things too wonderful for me, which I did not know" (Job 42:3).

Beethoven lived for a time in Vienna with a young dramatist named Grillparzer, a nervous, timid man. One day Grillparzer received an invitation to attend a reception in honor of a distinguished poet and dramatist. Despite his intense desire to meet the famous writer, Grillparzer declined the invitation. He explained to Beethoven, "I won't go. He knows too much for me. Suppose he asks me, 'Who or what is God?' I don't know, but *he* knows —and it would be horribly embarrassing not to be able to join in the conversation."

Tennyson's philosophizing on the "flower in the crannied wall" suggests that any being who could comprehend God fully would be more than human. He would be less than a mature human being, however, if he had no interest in exploring the concept of God.

Men in their relation to God must be somewhat like pets in their relation to us. If you have a dog, do you ever wonder how much he understands about you? There can be no doubt that he understands you in part. He knows he can trust you, while he must approach strangers questioningly. Yet you do strange things. You go away for days at a time; you never explain your vacations. You come home late, and you never explain why the porch is cold and the supper is delayed. Despite such handicaps to faith, your dog continues to have faith in you. He knows you are his friend, and he is loyal to you.

Men, being men, are destined to trust God, if at all, on the same limited basis of understanding. By their faith, many have made a true home of this universe.

From the primitive conception of the early Old Testament to the noble religion of the prophets and Jesus, the Bible is an extended history of how men have thought about God. The Nineteenth Psalm is often quoted as an exposition of two manifestations of God. The first half of the psalm deals with the world of astronomy: "The heavens are telling the glory of God." The second half deals with the God within: "The law of the Lord is perfect, reviving the soul." Kant, the German philosopher, was impressed by these two declarations, writing, "Two things fill the mind with ever new and increasing admiration and awe . . . : the starry heavens above and the moral law within." [1]

The various authors of the Bible did not limit their discovery of God to astronomy and to human nature. "The Lord bringeth the counsel of the nations to naught" is a statement regarding history. "The cedars of Lebanon which he planted" declares the place of God in botany. When David prayed "Create in me a clean heart, O God," he testified to the dependence of the human soul on the Something Above and Beyond.

The immensity of the problem of discovery challenges us. If it is true that to understand God means that we should understand the universe, it must be equally true that to understand the universe would be to understand God. Such understanding, in part at least, is entirely possible. The discovery of God is being achieved by prophets, poets, philosophers, psychologists, historians, and scientists. It is a discovery in which everyone may share.

If a person comes to me in sincerity and asks, "What is God? What do people mean when they talk about God?" I make three simple statements. At the risk of over-simplification, I avoid the big words that for centuries have delighted the scholars. Jesus showed how to discuss God in language combining popular intelligibility with pregnancy of meaning. I try to follow his example. Here are the statements:

1. God is your own best self.

Begin the search for God with what we know best—ourselves. Surely all of us are aware of two tendencies in our make-up. One is selfish, leading us to meanness, cruelty, and greed. The other is unselfish, directing us to kindness, helpfulness, and even self-sacrifice.

Abraham Lincoln gave expression to a universal experience when he said to Herndon, his law partner, "Billy, when I do right, I feel clean inside. When I do wrong, I feel like a sheep-killing dog."

Everyone knows how it feels to be "clean inside." Everyone knows how uncomfortable, how miserable is the aftermath of unkindness or any genuine sin. Something within each of us is dissatisfied with meanness and selfishness. Jesus, you remember, located the Kingdom of God within the human heart.

Begin thinking about God with your own experience. If you first think of God simply as your own best self, you will have no difficulty understanding or believing.

This God you have tested. You are acquainted with him. He has saved you from temptation. He has many times led you into nobility of thought and deed surprising even to yourself. It was of this best self, the God within, that Shakespeare was thinking when he had Polonius say to his son:

> This above all: to thine own self be true,
> And it must follow, as the night the day,
> Thou canst not then be false to any man.[2]

2. God is the good in humanity.

A human being should not find it too difficult to admit that every other human being also has a Best Self. Surely my nature is very similar to the nature of other normal human beings. Though this nature may be modified by the environmental factors of home, school, fatherland, religion, and occupation, I believe that the Best Self in me is duplicated in essence in every other normal human being.

God thus becomes in our thinking not only the Lord, the Father, or the Great Soul of our own personal lives, but the Spiritual Force in the universe uniting in noble purpose all human beings.

With regard to this idea of God there can be no atheism except the denial of brotherhood. When a man says, "I believe in God," he means also "I believe in the spiritual unity of the whole human family." Jesus used the familiar analogy of the home. He called God, Father; he called all men and women, brothers and sisters. Jesus combined the two commandments of love for God and love of neighbor into one rule of life.

As the belief in a personal Best Self does not deny the continued presence of contrary impulses, so the belief in a Common Best Self of All Humanity does not deny there is much in humanity that is evil. The principal difference between a religious person and an irreligious person lies in what each believes to be the proper destiny of man. The irreligious person sees in man only a superior animal. The religious person need not deny the animal ancestry of man, but he believes God resides in the heart of man.

To believe in God is, first, to dedicate your will to the supremacy of your best self; and, second, to dedicate your will to the solemn belief that humanity itself is at least equal to the goodness in your own life. We human beings simply cannot afford the heresy that God lives in us and our kind and in us only.

Even in periods of fear and suffering, when hate is grown faster than it can be understood, the believer in God stands firm in his devotion to human brotherhood. His faith in God and man is not a reed shaken by the wind. For him it is the Rock of Ages.

3. God is all that is dependable in the universe.

Anyone who observes this world soon learns of its dependability in many important aspects. The evidence resulting from observation is to many the occasion for belief in God. If we did not call this dependability God, we should have to call it Order, Cosmos, Regularity, Reliability, or some such descriptive name. The dependability is so remarkable, so invariable, that a sincere student's attitude in its presence is best termed worship.

In the moral realm the law of the universe is dependable. Note carefully the following statements of various moral laws selected from here and there in the Bible.

Judge not, that you be not judged.

All who take the sword will perish by the sword.

It is easier for a camel to go through the eye of a needle than for a rich man to enter the kingdom of God.

The love of money is the root of all evil.

The wicked shall depart to Sheol, all the nations that forget God.

There is no peace, says the Lord, for the wicked.

Hatred stirs up strife.

Pride goes before destruction.

The fear of the Lord is the beginning of wisdom.

These are not merely good memory verses. These verses are part of the moral code of the world. All should know them, for with regard to the moral law as well as the civil law, ignorance of the law excuses no one.

By discovery of the reliability of moral law, God has become better known to man. Through centuries of experience with life, man has come to know a great deal about his world-home. The moral law is part of the nature of God. As E. Stanley Jones wrote, "Men do not break the laws of God; they break themselves in the attempt." The product of such experience is respect for the dependability of God's laws.

Science is as important as theology in the discovery of God. Theology seeks God through faith and reason; science seeks God through test tube, microscope, telescope, and space vehicles. When all learning has been brought together, the unity of the universe becomes apparent. Science has become a tremendous aid to faith in God, for its continuous revelation of law and order from the atom to the solar system confirms the faith of the theologian in an ordered world.

For example, take the most awe-inspiring science of all —astronomy. We know that the stars do not change their positions with relation to one another. The Big Dipper and the Little Dipper are so dependable that in a modern planetarium their night life can be revealed for centuries either in the past or in the future. Go to the planetarium in New York, Chicago, or Pittsburgh:

> . . . Look at thy heavens, the work of thy fingers,
> The moon and stars which thou hast established. . . .
> (Ps. 8:3)

The limitless field of the heavens is so regulated that an astronomer can say to the star Vega, "Where were you on the night of October 12, 1492?" and be able to check on the reply. When Laplace, the French astronomer, reported that he had searched the skies with his telescope and had not discovered God, he was not being profound—he was merely being cute. The fact is that he found nothing but God.

Docks are built with confidence, for tides are predictable. Ventilating and refrigerating systems are designed with the assurance that hot air will be lighter than cold air tomorrow as today. In war and in peace water continues to boil at 100 degrees Centigrade under standard pressure. When pressure on a contained gas is increased, the volume always decreases in proportion unless the temperature changes; Boyle's Law is revelation of the changeless God. NaCl, sodium chloride, is table salt now as in the time of Moses. A thousand years hence four times four will equal sixteen.

Michael Pupin was one of the twentieth century's first great physicists. Note his reasoning: "We are faced with two alternatives: We can either believe that cosmos, the beautiful law and order, is simply the result of haphazard happenings, or that it is the result of a definite Intelligence. Now, which are you, as an intelligent being, going to choose? I choose to believe in the coordinating principle, the Divine Intelligence. Why? Because it is simpler. It is more intelligible. It harmonizes with my whole experience."

But we need such a synthesizing analogy as the following from Albert Schweitzer to harmonize all the preceding: "There is an ocean—cold water without motion. In this ocean, however, is the Gulf Stream, hot water flowing from the equator towards the Pole. Inquire of all scientists how it is physically imaginable that a stream of hot water flows between the waters of the ocean, which, so to speak, form its banks, the moving within the motionless, the hot within the cold: no scientist can explain it. Similarly, there is the God of love within the God of the forces of the universe—one with Him, and yet so totally different. We let ourselves be seized and carried away by that vital stream." [3]

If God is (1) our own best self, (2) the good in humanity, and (3) all that is dependable in the universe (item 3, of course, includes 1 and 2), few people can honestly consider themselves atheists. Elizabeth York Case was right when she declared:

> There is no unbelief;
> Whoever plants a seed beneath the sod
> And waits to see it push away the clod—
>   He trusts in God . . .
> Whoever says when clouds are in the sky
> 'Be patient, heart; light breaketh by and by'
>   Trusts the Most High. [4]

More atheists are made by narrow definitions than by lack of faith.

Faith in God, to be sure, does not deny the presence of evil or the reality of trouble. There is more to man than his Best Self. There is more to humanity than Goodness. There are elements in nature that are not predictable—the floods, the earthquakes, the epidemics.

These natural evils, let us acknowledge, are not wholly separate from man's stupidity and error. Man has had a share in the creation of floods and epidemics, and he may live, if he chooses, where earthquakes are remote possibilities.

Grief and pain remain, however, and we can understand them only as part of the scheme of human rotation on this planet—birth and death—with the attendant character development through sympathy and love.

The man who has truly found God in himself, in his neighbors, and in his world has found a home in the universe. He sings with conviction,

> This is my Father's world,
> And to my listening ears,
> All nature sings, and round me rings
> The music of the spheres. . . .
> This is my Father's world,
> He shines in all that's fair; . . .
> He speaks to me everywhere.[5]

In the universe of the believer, God is both Father and Mother, and all men and women are brothers and sisters.

This is the faith of Jesus. Jesus not only proclaimed this truth, but his life and death are the best evidence ever produced by the universe that at the heart of all things is the Father God. He who has seen Jesus has indeed seen God, whose nature he personified in human life.

The discovery of God, like the pursuit of culture, is the search of a lifetime. "We have but faith," wrote Tennyson, "a beam in darkness: let it grow." [6] A religious

person has a lifetime job (1) cultivating his own Best
Self, (2) trusting the God in others, and (3) finding God
in every cranny of the universe.[7]

> i thank You God for most this amazing
> day:for the leaping greenly spirits of
>   trees
> and a blue true dream of sky;and for
>   everything
> which is natural which is infinite which
>   is yes
>
> (i who have died am alive again today,
> and this is the sun's birthday;this is
>   the birth
> day of life and of love and wings:and
>   of the gay
> great happening illimitably earth)
>
> how should tasting touching
>   hearing seeing
> breathing any—lifted from the no
> of all nothing—human merely being
> doubt unimaginable You?
>
> (now the ears of my ears awake and
> now the eyes of my eyes are opened)[8]

RELIGION NEEDS
TO BE CLARIFIED

Here are accounts of two people in unhappy situations.

A mother whose son had been killed in battle far from the shores of his homeland wrote to a clergyman: "I never intend to step inside a church again. It has fooled me. It has lied to me. It has taught me to believe that God would take care of my boy and bring him back in safety if I prayed. I have prayed. My boy is dead. What do you have to say to me now? I hate God. He cannot be trusted."

An elderly woman, for many years teacher of a church-school class, expressed bewilderment to her class one Sunday morning: "All my life," she declared, "I have been the best Christian I know how to be. And look at me now—crippled with arthritis!"

Both of these unhappy women obviously understood religion to be *insurance against calamity*.

Whenever religion is understood as insurance against calamity, the way to frustration and eventual atheism has been opened. In the experiences summarized above, the basis of belief in God had been distorted and misunderstood. Prayer does not stop an enemy bullet, nor does Christian living immunize against arthritis.

No amount of religion guarantees that people will never suffer from burglary, assault, fire, accident, illness, or bereavement. No responsible interpreter of religious faith ever claimed that human beings will be trouble-free if they are sufficiently religious.

Why, then, do such sad experiences as those related above occur? Can it be that some people so wish for insurance against catastrophe that they grasp at religion without really trying to understand its limitations as well as its power?

This is possible. Americans are so insurance conscious that, to borrow the common expression, many are "insurance poor." We have insurance protection against fire, theft, storm, accident, illness, hospitalization, total disability, unemployment, death, and so forth.

But deep down we are not really satisfied with our insurance protection, which offers only financial recompense for damages, losses, or expenses. We want more than financial assistance *after* misfortune strikes. We want a cover-all insurance policy that will *prevent* fire, theft, accidents, illness—even death before, let us say, the age of 101.

"Tom," complained a young woman to her automobile insurance agent, "I'm not satisfied with this agency. You insured me against accidents, and I've had four in the past two months."

This is similar to the fallacy that caused the trouble in the cases cited earlier: religion understood to be insurance against serious trouble.

An army chaplain in wartime asked his church paper to print this blunt but necessary statement: "I wish people would stop writing about the soldiers who pray and have their prayers answered by not getting killed. Why do all the others get the wrong answers? . . . And what about the fathers and mothers and wives and children? . . . I am depressed by the writings of those who try to get other people to pray by telling them that you get what you want. People must learn to want what they get."

There can be no doubt that Jesus died in harmony with God and trusting God. Yet Christians cannot forget that in Gethsemane Jesus prayed for life, and the answer was death.

Perhaps we can clarify the confusion if we examine the origins. How is it, aside from an unconscious wish to insure against all catastrophe, that modern people could hold the superstitious belief that religion can prevent personal misfortune?

The answer is in the Bible. Shot through and through this book is the story of man's struggle with the "be-good-and-be-trouble-free" idea. The ancient Hebrew doctrine of human suffering was simple: God rewards righteousness with health and prosperity; he penalizes evil-doing with suffering. By the logic of this theory the only God-approved people are the healthy and the wealthy; God spares the righteous from danger, pain, and discomfort.

"A thousand may fall at your side, ten thousand at your right hand; but it will not come near you," asserts the author of Psalm 91 (v. 7).

Such confidence, of course, was not always sustained. Good men suffered. Evil men prospered. Bewilderment inevitably resulted. The result was the cry uttered even on Calvary: "My God, my God, why hast thou forsaken me? Why art thou so far from helping me . . .?" (Psalm 22:1).

On the other hand, wicked men who shamelessly ignored the laws of God were often observed to prosper, have large families, live long. Why—if the theory was correct? "Why do the wicked live, reach old age, and grow mighty in power? Their children are established in their presence, and their offspring before their eyes. Their houses are safe from fear, and no rod of God is upon them" (Job 21:7-9).

Eventually the thought arose that the *innocent* might suffer. The 53rd chapter of Isaiah, for example, makes this statement based upon the sufferings of Israel: "Surely he has borne our griefs and carried our sorrows; . . . he was wounded for our transgressions, he was bruised for our iniquities. . . ."

The old, primitive doctrine finally was flatly denied. "As he [Jesus] passed by, he saw a man blind from his birth. And his disciples asked him, 'Rabbi, who sinned, this man or his parents, that he was born blind?' Jesus answered, 'It was not that this man sinned, or his parents, but that the works of God might be made manifest in him'" (John 9:2-3).

In the Sermon on the Mount, Jesus made the new understanding abundantly clear: "Love your enemies and pray for those who persecute you, so that you may be sons of your Father who is in heaven; for he makes his sun rise on the evil and on the good, and sends rain on the just and the unjust" (Matt. 5:44-45).

St. Paul set the Christian doctrine on this subject in sharp focus: "*All* things work together for good to them that love God" (Rom. 8:28, *KJV*). The key word is the italicized word: *all*.

"Sam" Shoemaker, who had notable parish ministries in New York and Pittsburgh Episcopal churches, wrote about a minister friend of his who preached on this text one Sunday, after which a man in the congregation asked him if he felt he could live up to the text under any circumstances. The minister replied that he would certainly try.

Two days later, he went hunting with some men of his congregation. A gun was discharged accidentally, blinding the minister in both eyes. Later, at the hospital, he said his first thought out there in the woods when he realized he would never see again was the text of the previous Sunday morning: "All things work together for good to them that love God."

As best he could, he continued his ministry. Dr. Shoemaker made this comment on the years that followed: "All who know him consider his victory over his own misfortune the greatest sermon he ever preached. . . . He has not felt the least rebellion against God." [1]

To trust God is to believe it is worthwhile to base life firmly on moral principle without regard to rewards, punishments, or consequences. The good life, the religious life, the life of the soul, is its own adequate reward.

If anyone preaches the Christian good news by guaranteeing a trouble-free life on earth, or scares a convert into church with the horrors of a physical hell, his religion is on a low, primitive, sub-Christian level.

Christians have their share of human misery, which they bear with confidence in God and in their God-given power. Much suffering is part of the pattern of human life. J. B. Goode was right when he wrote:

> Who ne'er has suffered, he has lived but half.
> Who never failed, he never strove or sought.
> Who never wept is stranger to a laugh
> And he who never doubted, never thought.

Much of the trouble people experience, moreover, is their own fault:

> I made the cross myself whose weight
>   Was later laid on me.
> This thought is torture as I toil
>   Up life's steep Calvary. [2]

What can we expect of religion? Much, if we do not approach God as if he were the manager of a bargain basement.

God has not promised skies always blue,
Flower-strewn pathways all our lives through;
God has not promised sun without rain,
Joy without sorrow, peace without pain.

God has not promised we shall not know
Toil and temptation, trouble and woe;
He has not told us we shall not bear
Many a burden, many a care.

God has not promised smooth roads and wide,
Swift, easy travel, needing no guide;
Never a mountain, rocky and steep
Never a river, turbid and deep.

But God has promised strength for the day,
Rest for the labor, light for the way,
Grace for the trials, help from above,
Unfailing sympathy, undying love.[3]

8

PRAYER IS
FOR MODERN MAN

Is prayer a futile exercise in talking to oneself? Is prayer a selfish "gimme" device? Is prayer a superstitious type of pre-Marconi communication?

Or is prayer a helpful habit of intelligent moderns who shun superstition and who seek release through prayer from the "gimme" aspect of self?

Obviously, among modern men and women there are conflicting notions of prayer. To some, prayer belongs to the prescientific era of demon exorcism and to the primitive religion of fearful man placating angry gods. To many, prayer is merely a harmless but time-wasting exercise in self-deception by which autosuggestion is misunderstood as the ability of man to alter the will of God.

My position is that basic prayer is part of every complete life. Without the constant practice of prayer, it is not likely that any individual will ever understand the paradox of happiness.

My pilgrim's progress in the understanding of prayer began as soon as I could understand the household language. There was "grace before meat" both noon and evening, and there was "Now I lay me down to sleep" before getting into bed each night. I gave little thought either to my own daily recitation or to the brief ritual prayer that preceded the family meals. Yet I recall that there was something assuring and unifying about the prayers of my childhood.

A few years before his death, Joyce Cary, the English novelist, reflected on the prayers of his childhood and concluded: "Prayers were a primitive ritual of duty, establishing a mutual bond, conciliating mysterious powers. But they affirmed and confirmed in my mind, my idea of things, the faith with which every child is born, that there is goodness in the world, in life; that to know it is all the security, and the peace, that life can give. And this is a true faith." [1]

What is the essential meaning of prayer to the understanding adult of today, to the man or woman who is content to leave childish limitations behind, and who is determined to preserve everything of lasting value?

Consider ten sentences that follow, each beginning with the words *"Prayer is."* They express the meaning of prayer as it has developed in my experience through the years that have passed since childhood. Note these ten sentences as they appear.

Prayer is a yearning to be worthy of acceptance by God and man.

"Prayer is a wish turned heavenward," explained Phillips Brooks, the noted Episcopal clergyman of the last century.

To his family-prescribed evening prayer, Albert Schweitzer, the boy, added these words: "O heavenly father, protect and bless all things that have breath; guard them from all evil, and let them sleep in peace." [2] *Prayer is aspiration*—in young Schweitzer's case, aspiration of the purest, most unselfish type.

Nearly five hundred years ago an Italian named Pico

della Mirandola wrote an essay titled "Oration on the Dignity of Man." His thesis was that the Creator made most creatures to be "determinate"—fish to live in water, animals to crawl or walk, etc. But he maintained that man alone was made "indeterminate" because he was given the power of choice—to live as befits his spiritual ancestry or to live lower than any beast. *Prayer is the choosing process.*

A poem written around 1818 and found today in many Christian hymnals begins with these illuminating lines:

> *Prayer is the soul's sincere desire,*
> *Uttered or unexpressed . . .*

In this simple sentence James Montgomery stated a profound truth: Prayer is "felt," and it may or may not be spoken. Audibility is not required when a human being "turns a wish heavenward," aspires purely, struggles to choose the better part.

The husband who mumbles, "How could I have spoken so harshly to the woman I love?" is praying a prayer of bitter repentance.

The teacher who looks over a classroom filled with young life and muses, "I must try harder to understand them," is deep in prayer.

The father who watches his little daughter at play and resolves with grim determination, "By God, no harm will come to her," is praying earnestly, not swearing.

The surgeon who leaves a party early the night before an operation and goes to bed sober for the sake of another human being is living a life of prayer.

The executive prays sincerely when he says, "This is a hard decision. But I have to live with my conscience, and only one right decision is possible."

If *"Prayer is thinking toward God,"* as John Baillie of

Edinburgh wrote, prayer is as natural and as necessary as laughter and tears.

Prayer is man's secret weapon in his lifelong warfare with worry, fear, boredom, unhappiness, cowardice, temptation, evil, betrayal, disease, and finally death. But the purpose of prayer in the arsenal of man is not to change God. It is to change man.

"Not my will, but thine, be done," was the prayer of the Teacher whose disciples had asked, "Lord, teach us to pray."

Yes, prayer changes things—it changes people who pray. It puts them into a close relationship with God and with their companions of the human way. Without prayer it is doubtful whether happiness can ever be found under a burden of unhappiness.

An activity in itself, prayer is also an incentive to purposeful activity. Prayer is never a substitute for effort; it is an effort in itself, sometimes the most difficult a person ever experiences.

Prayer is the language of the soul. Prayer is the open window of the soul. Prayer is man at his best.

9

CHRISTIANITY
IS RELEVANT

Some people believe that Christianity is shockingly naive
with respect to the world as it is. They claim that Christians live in a never-never state like Browning's girlish
Pippa, who went about in the midst of evil and pain
singing:

> God's in his heaven—
> All's right with the world!

Voltaire's *Candide* has an analogous character named
Dr. Pangloss who survived the most terrible experiences,
during which he constantly affirmed: "All is for the best
in this best of all possible worlds."

There are people who wrongly interpret "God is love,"
"This is my Father's world," "Christ is risen" as indicating
that Christians innocently, blindly believe this to be a
near-perfect world. The American Association for the Advancement of Atheism, for example, once suggested that
the doxology be revised to read "Praise God from whom
all cyclones blow," as if religious people need to be reminded that suffering and evil exist.

In view of the centrality of the resurrection of Christ in Christian doctrine, it could be considered strange that the cross, not the open tomb, is the symbol of faith. But from the earliest days of the Christian movement, followers of Jesus have chosen the cross more than any other symbol to represent the basic significance of their faith. They have done this in full knowledge that the cross on which Jesus died was not gold or brass or platinum, that it was not overlaid with precious jewels, that it was in fact a crude, ugly, hurriedly constructed wooden cross to which an innocent man was brutally nailed and which, before the man had uttered the words "It is finished," was splattered with blood.

How, then, did the notion arise that Christians choose to see only the good in the world, that the followers of Jesus are starry-eyed in their idealism?

The explanation can easily be made too simple, but certainly one reason for the misconception is the utopian liberalism that strongly influenced Christian thinking during the first third of the twentieth century.

Prior to that time and the closing years of the preceding century, the common concept of human progress was what is sometimes called the ladder theory. To improve, according to this understanding, man had to climb—and he did not always choose to climb; there were times when he actually took downward steps. Religious people envisioned God high above the ladder entreating man to climb and stretching forth a helping hand. But the decision to ascend, descend, or stand still was always man's.

Then the escalator idea was invented. According to this theory, progress is inevitable; you can see it in history for six thousand years, and you can anticipate the sweet day of perfection. Tennyson felt this surging optimism and affirmed the new faith in stirring lines like these.

> . . . Arise and fly
> The reeling Faun, the sensual feast;
> Move upward, working out the beast,
> And let the ape and tiger die.[1]

The fallacy was that men mistook the possibility of progress for inevitability.

Perhaps this philosophical and theological fallacy was an outgrowth, in part at least, of the nineteenth-century doctrine of biological evolution. If the continuous working of evolution has developed higher and higher forms of biological life, why (as Herbert Spencer thought) should we not expect the survival of the fittest in the moral realm to evolve higher and higher forms both of the individual human being and of human society?

No doubt the comfortable Pax Britannica which dominated world history for the century before World War I also contributed to the belief that major wars and wanton massacres belonged to the outgrown past. Victor Hugo was so hopeful about the twentieth century that he predicted, "In the twentieth century war will be dead, the scaffold will be dead, hatred will be dead, dogmas will be dead, frontier boundaries will be dead; man will live." In Chicago, U.S.A., a magazine was founded with the hopeful title: *Christian Century*.

From about the time Walter Rauschenbush published *Christianity and the Social Crisis* in 1907 until the black night of Hitlerism overcame the earth in 1939, the so-called social gospel increasingly influenced Christian thinking. During these years, churchmen sang "Brighten the Corner Where You Are" and proclaimed the perfect Kingdom of God on earth in the near future. "The World for Christ in This Generation!" became the battle cry. Away with war, poverty, economic injustice, alcoholism, bigotry, hatred, *now*!

And then Hitler brought the flimsy edifice of phony optimism toppling to the ground. When the dust and smoke had cleared, six million non-Christian men, women, and children had been systematically murdered by a nation that for a thousand years had called itself Christian, and literally tens of millions had died in the worldwide struggle.

The hell through which the peoples of the earth passed between 1939 and 1945 ended with no promise of peace or happiness. Nuclear weapons, one of which could wipe out an entire city—as another nation with Christian roots had twice demonstrated—were left dangling over the life of every person on the planet. Moreover, the two new superpowers, in a mutual attempt to encircle each other, produced a war that has been alternately cold and hot and which all but destroyed the peace of mind of an entire generation.

In the process, Christian thinking has been put back on the track. The social gospel, though helpful in many ways, proved to be a temporary escape from the long-held view that life can never guarantee immunity to sin or suffering, now or a millennium from now. The long view of man on this earth eliminates the possibility of surprise when unhappiness is discovered or experienced.

Our fathers sang:

> Lead me through the vale of shadows,
>   Bear me o'er life's fitful sea.

* * *

> While life's dark maze I tread,
>   And griefs around me spread . . .

* * *

> I'm but a stranger here; Heaven is my home.

The world has been thought of traditionally in Christian circles as so essentially bad that many Roman Catholics have felt obliged to withdraw and live apart in monasteries or convents. In the past many Protestants regarded worldliness as so evil that they sought to escape by avoiding the theater, popular forms of amusement, and even by forswearing jewelry and decorative clothing. An ancestor of mine confessed in a Sunday afternoon class meeting that she was guilty of worldliness—she was wearing a ruffle on her petticoat!

This attitude, rather than that of the departed Pollyanna era with its corner-brightening religion, is generally consistent with two thousand years of Christian history. Human progress is not by escalator with perpetual upward and onward thrust. It is by ladder, and it requires slow, painful climbing; one may go up or down. To the Christian, the ladder concept is not complete without an understanding of the forgiving grace and the upward pull of a Father God.

Let no one conclude that the social gospel has made no worthwhile contribution to the Christian fellowship, either in the United States, where its influence has been most powerful, or in the rest of the world. The social gospel has made three contributions of lasting value to the Christian cause.

1. It ended the shameful heresy that Christian faith can be applied only to an individual; applied religion is now accepted as possible for any area of social concern when enough people are willing to use it.

2. It ended the silly heresy, once widely held among Protestants, that pleasure is sinful.

3. It ended the frightful heresy, also held by many Protestants during three hundred years of church history, that appreciation of the beautiful in stained glass

windows, church architecture, and organ music is idolatrous and evil.

In short, the world is not as promising as the liberals thought, nor as hopeless as the orthodox maintained. Extremes on both sides have been disproved by time and history. The world is not all resurrection. But neither is it all crucifixion.

The capacity of human nature for both good and evil has been proved to be virtually limitless; manifestations of either should never surprise anyone. Judas' betrayal, though it pained Jesus, did not surprise him.

The paradox of happiness involves acceptance of human nature as it is, a nature that can amaze with high spiritual achievement as well as with base degradation. Human nature is always expressing itself in unexpected ways, but the really wise beneficiary, observer, or victim is never totally surprised, "Even the most sadistic and destructive man is human," Erich Fromm reminds us, "as human as the saint." [2]

Erich Remarque, in *A Time to Love and a Time to Die*, devised a good example of this principle when he described the killing of a trusting soldier by a man assumed to be harmless and for whose life he had just fought a fellow soldier.

In *The Adventures of Huckleberry Finn*, Mark Twain tells about the betrayal of Jim, a runaway Negro slave, by two men who had been companions and were assumed to be friends. Thinking, as Huck said, "till I wore my head sore," he was crushed "because they could have the heart to serve Jim such a trick as that, and make him a slave again all his life, and amongst strangers, too, for forty dirty dollars." [3]

The Christian, though somewhat fearful of the world's evil, and inclined to be wary of even its most intelligent inhabitants, can nevertheless live with profound peace of mind and joyous acceptance of things as they are. Against the darkness that is undeniably part of the world scene, he accepts Christ as the god-man, the man without evil, the man whose entire motive was love, the man whose life on earth produced the faith: "Light is come!"

As the nature of man would cause us to expect, the darkness attempted to put out the light. On Good Friday there was indeed darkness on earth.

But today the light of Christ shines through the lives of all those who welcome it. It shines through every true Christian and every genuine Christian church.

When the relevancy of Christianity is questioned, remember the scene in John Masefield's *The Trial of Jesus* in which the wife of Pilate and a Roman soldier talk following the crucifixion.

"Do you think He is dead?" she asks.

"No, lady, I don't," is the reply.

"Then where is He?" is the next question.

"Loose in the world, Lady, where no one can stop His truth!"

PART III

The Practice of Happiness

10

LIFE IS A
HARD-HAT AREA

"Hard-Hat Area—Do Not Enter!"

So read a sign at the entrance to a construction project. But I observed that despite the sign, many men entered the construction area every working day—and necessarily.

The men, of course, were hard-hat construction workers. They recognized the dangers involved in high-rise construction projects, and they knew how to go about their work with a maximum of protection and a minimum of fear. As both symbol and means of safety, each man wore a steel helmet designed to protect him from sudden danger.

Other kinds of people work in other kinds of hard-hat areas: firemen, policemen, physicians, nurses, mine rescue teams, men in military service, airplane pilots, etc.

In a larger sense all of us spend our lives in a hard-hat area—*life itself*. We never know when we may be hit by unkindness, ingratitude, jealousy, prejudice, hatred, envy, financial loss, unemployment, accident, illness, bereavement, or death.

There are two ways of reacting to the realization that life, all of it, is an area of constant hazard.

One way is to avoid as much of life as possible. The

inhibited, the timid, the cowardly are tempted to bypass as much of life as they can. So they avoid people for fear of being hurt, avoid responsibility for fear of being criticized, avoid ambition for fear of failing, avoid hope for fear of disappointment, and avoid attempts at friendship for fear of being rebuffed.

There are, it must be evident, only two means of complete escape by which human beings can avoid the burdens of living. One is suicide. The other is insanity.

Either may follow refusal or inability to enter the wide circle of life boldly with a maximum of protection and a minimum of fear. Suicide or insanity is the logical and final stage of retreat from life.

The second possible way of reacting to the reality of life is to put on the hard hat of faith in life's possibilities and to challenge life. This means to give life all you have. "Take the whole armor of God, that you may be able to withstand in the evil day, and having done all, *to stand*" (Eph. 6:13), advised St. Paul, who practiced what he preached.

No man knows when he undertakes something worthwhile whether he will succeed. A mother bears a child not knowing whether the child will become a blessing or a curse. A man establishes a business not knowing whether it will make him rich or bankrupt. A surgeon begins a lifesaving operation not knowing whether the result will be life or death. Clearly, the best approach to life is to undertake boldly what ought to be done and to do so with maximum protection and minimum fear.

There is one fear that is totally honorable and defensible: the fear of failure to do one's duty. Other fears usually have nothing to do with honor or character. We fear illness, but illness is seldom dishonorable. We fear poverty, but poverty need not be dishonorable. We fear the failure of our efforts along many lines, but failure is not dishonorable if the goal was justifiable and the effort proportionate. We fear death, but death except in cowardice or neglect of duty is not dishonorable.

The answer to fear is faith and courage—the hard-hat elements of maximum protection. "If to do were as easy as to know what were good to do . . . ," sighed Portia to Nerissa.[1] But in difficult situations doing is not as easy as knowing.

John Galsworthy observed that courage is more important than love. But courage is an aspect of love. Faith, hope, and love combine to supply the courage that transforms the wish into the act, the prayer into the answer, the creed into the deed, the vision into the accomplishment. Calvary completed the Sermon on the Mount.

"Happiness at its deepest and best," wrote Dr. Fosdick, "is not the portion of a cushioned life which never struggled, overpassed obstacles, bore hardships, or adventured in sacrifice for costly aims. A heart of joy is never found in luxuriously coddled lives, but in men and women . . . who have tempered their souls in fire."[2]

The contrast between two elderly women, "equally devout by conventional standards," was pointed out by Reinhold Niebuhr. Both women understood that they faced death. As their pastor, Dr. Niebuhr visited them regularly. One woman wanted to hear psalms of praise and gratitude and talked a great deal about her wonderful daughters, both graduate nurses. The other "was a fever of anxiety and resentment. She recounted all her virtues with the implication that it was unjust for a righteous woman to suffer her pains."

Concluded Dr. Niebuhr, "I learned from the one that gratitude is the natural response of a life lived in faith as trust in the goodness of life. I learned from the other that faith is frequently corrupted by childish peevishness about the lack of special favors for the righteous."[3]

"Affliction does so color a life," said a sympathetic visitor to a paralyzed girl.

"Yes, and I propose to choose the color," was the affirmative reply.[4]

"To choose the color" of our reaction is sometimes all we can do when disaster occurs. To do less is to double the misfortune. To do so successfully is to live as happily as is probably good for man.

"Happiness is a habit," says Phyllis Diller, the comedienne. Neither Plato nor Marcus Aurelius nor Ralph Waldo Emerson ever uttered a more profound truth.

11

RATIONAL FEAR
IS MAN'S FRIEND

The notion that fear is bad should be rejected. There are sensible fears—justifiable, rational, useful fears.

Within limits, the fear of fires, for example, is sensible. Because there is real danger that a house may catch fire, precautions are taken when a house is planned, when it is built, when it is furnished, when it is painted. Realizing that fires sometimes happen even when all known precautions have been observed, property owners invest in fire insurance, not because they are pessimists but because they are realists.

The controlled kind of fear that leads to wise precautionary measures is one of mature man's most helpful qualities. It prevents the kind of reckless speed on the highway that maims and kills. It causes people to put money aside for illness, unemployment, retirement. It is responsible for health examinations and for precautionary inoculations.

This kind of fear is part of man's natural armor of defense. It calls for no apology. It needs no defense.

The difference between rational fear and irrational fear is apparent. Irrational fear is displayed by the person who is so fearful of fire that he will never sleep above the ground floor anywhere he goes; the person who is so fearful of enclosed space that he will never enter an elevator; the person who is so fearful of accidental death that he will not ride the bus to work; the person who is so fearful of being murdered that each night he barricades every door and window of his house.

Such fears have normal bases. But in these sad cases fears have become painfully abnormal. After all, a person can have only so much security in life. We could wrap ourselves like cocoons, hide from life, and still suffer from all the shocks and disasters that man is heir to. We simply must accept risks as part of existence.

For the person who is able to control his reactions and emotions, the answer to foolish fear is growth toward full maturity. The answer for the others, those who are literally sick with frightening phobias, lies in treatment by specialists in psychiatry or in disorders of the spirit.

Childhood fears frequently vanish with the attainment of maturity. "The green-eyed monster with the thirteen tails" and "the goblin'll get you if you don't watch out" become part of childish lore along with happy experiences of Santa Claus and holiday trips to Grandma's. Crossing a crowded street, facing a strange dog, confronting the darkness—these can be formidable tasks for "little" people.

Fortunate is the person who progresses from childhood to adulthood with his juvenile fears left behind him. But unfortunate is the adult who exchanges his childish fear of the stranger who will cut his ear off for an equally foolish adult fear of illness, high altitude, death, or loneliness. To the extent that such fears exceed the reasonable or the tolerable, the rational adult will fight them with boldness of spirit.

The real test of mature reason and strength, however, comes when the worst actually happens, when a reasonable fear proves true and nothing can be done to stop it—the fire really happens, the crash actually occurs, the doctor cannot help, the crime is done.

If frustration follows, the effect of disaster will surely be greater disaster. If the survivor lies there, like the character in Edgar Allan Poe's "The Pit and the Pendulum," paralyzed by shock and frustration, merely awaiting inevitable doom, he has failed the test.

But what can a man or a woman do when the worst has happened?

He or she can hold on—*and hold on a little longer!*

A happy young New York couple, planning to be married on Friday, went shopping on Tuesday. The exuberant bride-to-be turned toward her fiancé as she stepped off the curb into the busy avenue and was struck by an automobile. On Friday there was a funeral instead of a wedding.

The bereaved young man spent Friday evening with thoughts of taking his life. But there were things he felt he should attend to, and he decided to postpone the end until Sunday.

When Sunday came, something drew him to the church where the wedding was to have been held. The sermon that morning was titled "The Breaking Point." "It is always possible to hold on a little longer," the minister confidently maintained, and he cited examples of hurt but brave people who had done just that.

According to a letter received by the minister a month later, the sermon caused a suicide to be delayed and later given up entirely.

There is not a single terrifying experience any of us could have that men and women have not had to endure again and again from the beginning of time. There is no unique or unusual hardship known among men.

To paraphrase Elijah, "We are no better than our fathers" (I Kings 19:4). The lot of previous generations, truthfully, was no easier or harder than ours. Circumstances and environment change, but basic human problems are constant through all time.

The "serenity" prayer by Reinhold Niebuhr arouses universal response, for it brings wisdom and nobility of aspiration to all kinds of problems. Here it is in the 1943 version: "God, give us grace to accept with serenity the things that cannot be changed, courage to change the things that should be changed, and the wisdom to distinguish the one from the other."

One of the earliest and hardest lessons we learn in life is that no matter how much we try we cannot always have things our way. When I was a college sophomore, I wrote for delivery at a state contest an oration on the subject "The Master of Destiny." The concluding words, I confess, were these: "Let us resolve to be the captains of our lives, the masters of our destinies." The sophomore uttered these brave words without reservation or doubt.

During the same school year the dean of our college, an outstanding English professor, wrote a poem comparing men with pebbles pushed along by a rushing brook.

Both of us missed the point, I now believe. No man is really the master of his destiny, as I believed at nineteen. But no man need be a pebble pushed helplessly and aimlessly by the brook, as the professor believed.

With happiness as an established habit, a person will be satisfied to control as much of life as he can and to accept the rest.

In the process we learn life's majors and minors. Here are things that really matter: our loves and our friendships; our concerns and our crusades; our sense of beauty and trust; our faith that however life goes with us, the prophets and the saints have shown us how to win and how to lose, how to live and how to die.

12

OPPOSITION
CAN BE MANAGED

The man who wrote, "If possible, so far as it depends upon you, live peaceably with all" (Rom. 12:18), was in one scrap after another all his life. Read his life story in the New Testament and then marvel at his advice to "live peaceably with all."

Perhaps the scrappy writer, who never dreamed he would some day be called a saint, retired for the night after writing the last clause of the sentence: "live peaceably with all." How could he sleep after penning such an impossible preachment? Had he lived "peaceably with all"?

So Paul arose and added a vital conditional clause: "so far as it depends upon you." Then he slept.

In the morning he read again his two-part counsel: "So far as it depends upon you, live peaceably with all." But he added a weary second condition: "if possible."

Paul knew that no one can live without conflict. It simply is not possible—whether you are president of the United States or merely a next-door neighbor in Middle America. You are bound to do something, say something, write something, or just think something that will create opposition and conflict.

The Bible, a faithful mirror of humanity, opens with conflict in the Garden of Eden and murder in the first family. With the exception of the Book of Ruth, an island of love and loyalty in a sea of hatred and betrayal, every book in the Bible tells of conflict among men.

Surely Jesus would have lived "peaceably with all" if any man could. He went about "doing good," led by his conscience and his judgment. He harmed no one.

But carping criticism of his talk and his conduct soon developed into opposition. He had eaten with people who were less than perfect, his disciples had pulled grain off the stalks on the Sabbath when they were hungry, he had healed a man on the day when no work was to be done, he had assumed too much authority for one not rabbinically trained—so the critics screamed. And the result was a crescendo of opposition that in three years reached the full violence of crucifixion.

It is not possible to live without conflict. It is possible, though, to understand opposition and to develop techniques for dealing with it.

Sometimes opposition arises from a perfectly sincere and honest **difference in viewpoint.** Emerson spoke one Sunday morning from the pulpit of a rural church whose minister disagreed with everything the distinguished visitor said. The minister closed the service with this brief prayer: "We beseech Thee, O Lord, to deliver us from ever hearing any more such nonsense as we have just listened to from this sacred desk."

But opposition did not turn into conflict. When a worried member of the church asked Emerson what he thought of the minister, he remarked calmly, "The minister seems a very conscientious, plain-spoken gentleman."

Sometimes **misunderstanding** is the cause of trouble

between people. If the people involved are well adjusted emotionally and spiritually, a straightforward explanation ordinarily clears up the problem. When, for instance, my wife and I were on a vacation in the West, one of us (it would not be gallant to say which one) failed to show up for a full hour after we had agreed to meet at a certain place. When we were finally reunited, the air was a bit tense—until we discovered that one of us had set his watch for the local time and one had not. This was a simple, easily corrected case of misunderstanding.

Sometimes envy produces opposition, and envy is difficult to deal with. When success eludes a man or woman in matters of career, popularity, income, romance, looks, or anything else, envy of the person who has what the failure lacks is never surprising. This kind of envy is harmless so long as it remains incidental, secondary, so long as it does not build up to a self-defeating frustration.

But when envy gets out of hand it can be really murderous. Unable or unwilling to build himself up, the envious person may devilishly seek ways to tear down the object of his envy. An easy, obvious way is to tell lies. From this beginning there is a familiar pattern of escalation that can lead to physical harm to the object of envy.

I recall a wonderful college girl who was popular with both faculty and students—and, more remarkably, with both boys and girls. Then it happened. Malicious gossip began and spread. The cause, it was finally learned, was the envy of a mousy little creature who could never have either the brains or the beauty of the girl she was determined to destroy.

"Anyone can sympathize with the sufferings of a friend," observed Oscar Wilde, "but it requires a very fine nature to sympathize with a friend's success."

When ambition causes conflict, the source is usually

evident. In the political arena rivals slug it out in full view of the spectators.

But sometimes the "sterner stuff" of which Anthony spoke at the funeral of Caesar is less apparent. There may be four sopranos in a choir, for example, and each may be figuratively cutting the throats of all the others because of unrecognized ambition to be the best—or possibly the only—soprano in the group. This type of opposition, too, is not easy to handle.

Sometimes there is **opposition nobody can explain.** The quatrain written on an Oxford University wall long ago by a student who could not endure Professor Fell is the classic expression of this kind of opposition:

> I do not like thee, Dr. Fell,
> The reason why I cannot tell.
> I only know, and know full well,
> I do not like thee, Dr. Fell.

It must have been this same sort of mysterious dislike that caused the lifeguard to explain why he was resigning by saying: "I don't like the kind of people I am saving." Perhaps someone would have commented, "You don't have to be a cannibal to get fed up with people."

Why do we seem to have an instinctive dislike for certain people? Is it possible that there is such a thing as incompatibility of body chemistry? Can it be that the man to whom we react negatively reminds us unconsciously of another man who long ago grabbed a toy from us? Or can it be that the person we dislike for no apparent reason first appeared to dislike us? In every case of unexplained hostility there is an explanation. It is worth hunting for.

The person with a basically happy outlook on life knows

not to expect life without opposition or conflict. Such a life may be possible somewhere, sometime; it is not possible on earth. But *meeting opposition without fear or regret is possible.*

The first step in handling opposition is to *make sure our own motives are right.* Human beings, like nations, find it nearly impossible to convict themselves. "We" are pure, righteous, blameless. "They" are impure, wicked, guilty.

So long as this self-deception lasts, there is little opportunity to understand the conflict or to deal with it. Even if we are convinced that all the blame rests on the other side, there is always the probability that with us some reaction of impatience, resentment, or hatred has occurred.

An elderly black elevator operator said when I was in her city to speak for a Brotherhood Week occasion, "Our people need this brotherhood talk, too—when you're hated you hate back." But while a person is hating back, he is in no condition to handle opposition—certainly not if his aim is to restore harmony.

The second step in dealing with conflict, then, is to *make sure we do not catch our opponent's hatred.* If this happens, we have lost our balance and are not in a position to think clearly or plan logically; emotion has the upper hand. Dr. Fosdick described the condition thus: "How like we human beings are to dogs! For one dog barks and the other barks back and the first barks more loudly and the second becomes more noisy still, in a mounting crescendo of hostility. So one man excused his terrier to the exasperated owner of another. 'After all,' he said, 'the dog is only human.' " [1]

The third step in handling opposition has already been implied: *Stand ready for the renewal of friendship and harmony—even if it is refused.*

Harry Overstreet strongly recommended that people in conflict consider the alternatives other than the first inclinations to fight or to take flight. Frequently these are the first reactions to opposition, but they are likely to be emotional and unthinking.

When we are attacked, we are, in most cases, disposed to *fight or flight*, as Dr. Overstreet pointed out.[2] A third "F" was prescribed by Jesus of Nazareth: *forgiveness*—not once, but seventy times seven times, as phrased in the Oriental hyperbole of which the Master was fond. He was right: Never in this world was hatred ever ended by hatred.

As a last step, if every other has failed and the conflict continues, *one can manage* without the desired reconciliation *if* he does not feel sorry for himself, *if* he does not assume the role of martyr to the evil of another man, and *if* he does not accumulate frustrated rage with its inevitable penalties of headaches, ulcers, and other more serious ills that emotional maladjustments are almost certain to produce in time.

To men and women in turmoil I have said this scores of times: *Peace is always relative.* To be alive is to have conflicts. Only the dead have finished with them.

But only the devils of earth do not wish to live peaceably with all men. The rest of us go on trying.

13

MARRIAGE IS A
MATTER OF FAITH

Sensational talk about the declining popularity of monogamy in the United States is ending. No wonder! Facts never existed to support wild predictions that widespread acceptance of alternative marriage patterns was at hand.

Sure, the divorce rate of one for every four marriages continues, and no doubt many married couples not considering divorce hardly regard their marriages as successful. But most divorced people remarry within four years, let it be noted—a pattern called serial monogamy if repeated several times. (A *New Yorker* cartoon illustrates the beginning of serial monogamy: *"Darling! Our first marriage!"* a young bride says to her equally young husband as they leave the home of a justice of the peace.)

Shacking up, trial marriage, cohabitation, adultery are as old as history. Mate swapping (within marriage!) has a new twist in our time, but one of the Ten Commandments deals with lusting for a neighbor's wife. Even communes are revivals of earlier attempts to be different, and they are sparse except to a limited extent in California and New York. Moreover, monogamy is frequently the rule in communes. Rare is a New Mexico group in which

"Everyone is married to everyone. The children are every-one's." [1]

"Marriage: It's Still Popular in the U.S."—a headline in the *New York Times*—was not news to most Americans. The story reported a federal statistical study showing that in the last eighty years the percentage of Americans over fourteen who married increased steadily from one-half to more than two-thirds.[2]

Anne Roiphe, termed by *Vogue* "a woman who has paced with the vanguard in the Women's Movement," believes that "sexual change, freedom, opportunity, and choice are only the brighter sides of loneliness, isolation, thinness of contact." "In fact," she proclaims, "human beings, male and female, still seem to need a mate, a bed to share, someone to raise children with, someone to love even if you have a cold, lost your job, or had a nightmare; and the world is so full of nightmares it's good to have someone to wake with, to hold on to, to remember last year with and make plans for next." In marriage, she concludes, "People can build a shelter for themselves instead of a prison." [3]

A director of the Palo Alto Mental Research Institute, William J. Lederer, cites these findings:

People who have good marriages enjoy better health and live longer than those who have discordant marriages or who remain single.

People who have good marriages usually experience a higher measure of economic comfort than those who have bad marriages.

The children of parents who have good marriages are more inclined to have good marriages of their own.

The conclusion is obvious: A good marriage provides a

very efficient, pleasant, and profitable way for most people to live.[4]

The problem, then, is how to achieve a *good* marriage. Those who have found marriage the basis for generally happy living demonstrate certain common characteristics —though there are exceptions.

1. Most happily married couples married after, not during, the height of romantic intoxication.

Infatuation is a common state for two people who have just fallen in love. It is shown in physical symptoms such as increased respiration and heartbeat, flushed cheeks, difficulty of concentration except on the love object. Such a condition may eventually level out to a lengthy—possibly lifetime—love relationship, or it may splutter out in dying embers of emotion.

But during the euphoric mood of infatuation, human judgment is utterly undependable. Dr. Louis E. Bisch, a New York psychiatrist, advises that "romance blinds people, obsesses them, deludes them. Marry, of course, but first get over your attack of love sickness."[5] This once-popular song expresses the mood of infatuation:

I couldn't realize what a pair of eyes and a baby smile
    could do;
I can't sleep, I can't eat,
I never knew a single soul could be so sweet.[6]

George Bernard Shaw called marriage "the most licentious institution on earth." The place of sex in an enduring marriage relationship can be understood better late in life than at the outset of a marriage, but "licentious" is not the right word. Since "love" in the English language is a vague and gravely overworked word, the result for some people is confusion regarding marriage.

The ancient Greeks had three words for love, each expressing a phase of adult life. One word means spiritual love, a religious quality. Another means friendship, brotherly love. The third means sexual love.

In a good marriage all three kinds of love flow freely. There is sexual love, and while its expressions vary with the decades, it remains to the end. When Ann Landers said "My husband is my best friend, and I am his," she gave testimony to the second kind of married love. The place of spiritual love in a good marriage is beautifully expressed by the grandfather in Anne Morrow Lindbergh's *Dearly Beloved*:

> But happiness wasn't anything you found, in marriage or in life, for that matter. . . . Marriage, in his experience, wasn't primarily concerned with happiness. It was too intent on something else—*love*, he supposed. . . . *Ti voglio bene*, the Italian phrase, was closer to the meaning: I wish what is best for you. If you wanted the best for the other person, everything else followed, happiness too.[7]

2. Most happily married couples married at the right time. Impulse marrying, like impulse buying, is reckless. Survival of the infatuation period is not in itself sufficient assurance that the time to marry has arrived, though it is a significant milestone in that direction.

A bride-to-be asked a minister if he would omit from her marriage ceremony the words "till death do us part." "My answer," he replied, "depends entirely upon your intention. Neither of us can know today how you and Bob will feel concerning each other ten years, twenty years, from now. But if it is not at this moment your intention and earnest desire to spend your lives together as husband and wife, I will not only not delete 'till death do us part' from the ceremony—I will not perform the ceremony."

"So long as you both shall *love*" has been proposed as replacement for the traditional promise of permanence in matrimony. In view of the divorce statistics, this substitution may appear realistic and honest. But if a bride and groom accept each other only tentatively—on approval—the chances of marital durability are seriously diminished.

The first American surgeon to perform a heart transplant, Dr. Adrian Kantrowitz, believes human beings should live to be 125 years old. This belief prompted a silly question from a behavioral scientist, a question that did not arise from a happy marriage. He asked, "How many people who are married would have been willing to say 'til death do us part' if they had known marriage would last 100 years?"

Those who married the right partners at the right time want nothing better than to share both happiness and unhappiness with their chosen mates as long as possible—a century is too short for really happy husbands and wives.

> "Love while you may,"
> The poets say.
> Love's season is brief.
> The pink of May
> Has scarcely burst
> Before the first
> Red leaf of autumn
> Is blown away.
>
> Moments of singing,
> Of kissing and clinging
> Ride on the wind
> Like milkweed fluff,
> Like the russet leaf.
> Love's season is brief:
> Only a lifetime . . .
> Never enough.[8]

Not all marriages are of the romantic, made-in-heaven type, we must admit. Many are compromises that appear to the participants to be the best solution to genuine needs and problems: craving for companionship, desire to get away from the family nest, need for financial support, hunger for home cooking, fear of living alone, reluctance because of social pressure to be a life-long single man or woman.

In any case, future happiness is likely to be enhanced if a marriage is not rushed into. Counselors believe two years is about the right length for most engagements, but circumstances may indicate longer or shorter "getting-to-know-you" periods. Separation is the best test for probable compatibility. Is the thought of absence genuinely saddening? Is the thought of reunion like the return of sunlight after rain?

3. **Most happily married couples married husbands and wives very much like themselves.**

Opposites attract, sometimes, but only superficially. It is the conclusion of most marriage advisers that opposites, however interesting as exotic creatures, are poor marriage risks. The more a bride and groom have in common, the better are their chances of success in marriage.

In most cases, therefore, whites should marry whites; blacks should marry blacks; Catholics should marry Catholics; Protestants, Protestants; Jews, Jews; Japanese, Japanese; Americans, Americans; college-educated, those with comparable education.

All of us can cite examples of "mixed" marriages that are successful beyond a doubt, and none of us would deny the right of human beings to choose their mates freely. But after this principle has been expressed and accepted, the fact remains that society imposes extra burdens on those who marry partners significantly different from themselves.

So far we have discussed prerequisites for happy marriages. But even happy marriages can be unhappy at times. No matter how well-adjusted a man and a woman are to each other's interests, habits, and personalities, inevitably there will be differences of opinions. There will be criticisms and arguments—mild or severe.

Because of this fact, the subject of marriage belongs in any analysis of the paradox of happiness. Those of us who would like our marriages to last a hundred years must admit that we have come to this attitude on the basis of understanding, accommodation, and ever-growing love. We have created a lasting marriage of mutual happiness out of the discarded possibilities of unhappiness.

Before a husband and wife decide to move their differences to the divorce court, they owe it to their dreams—and to their children, if any—to ask seriously whether each has made a reasonable effort to make the marriage a success. If remarriage is intended, they might ponder the sentiment of a French writer a century ago who compared the marriage failure with "the wretched fiddler who demands another violin, hoping that a new instrument will yield the melody he knows not how to play."

Here are questions that should be faced by every person caught in the whirlpool of a marriage crisis.

1. Have I believed honestly that marriage is a cooperative partnership of two separate but equal individuals?

2. Have I given as much to my marriage as I have expected from it?

3. Have I given justifiable excuse for jealousy?

4. Have I generally maintained a cheerful attitude?

5. Have I been enthusiastic about the intimacies of marriage without denying my partner the right to privacy in other personal matters?

6. Have I been too sensitive about little grievances?

7. Have I been mature and sensible about money matters?

8. Have I practiced cleanliness and reasonable tidiness?

9. Have I been kind and tactful in conversation?

10. Have I made a serious effort to get along with my spouse's family and friends?

Abiding faith in one's marriage partner comes from deep personal *respect*, not from sexual performance, earning power, appearance, academic degrees, or ancestry. Respect is the overwhelming acceptance of a partner that accompanies a good love affair and that assures a happy life together. Every husband and every wife has certain habits, mannerisms, and limitations that are not altogether pleasing to his or her mate. But if the husband or wife merits basic respect, love will learn to overlook the details.

James Thurber recorded this: "A lady of 47 who has been married 27 years and has six children described love to me—'Love is what you've been through with somebody.'" Exactly!

At the age of eighty, a loving, grateful husband talked about married life this way: "If someone had told me when I was ten that there was something called sex that was more interesting than chocolate ice cream sodas, I would have thought him crazy. And if someone had told me when I was sixty that there is something called understanding that can bring two people closer than sex, I would have thought him crazy."

When fearful young people talk of a marriage contract as if it abolishes freedom and establishes lifelong servitude, they should ponder these words of Dr. John Nef of the University of Chicago: "Freedom consists in choosing the right slavery. The true road to freedom is the road of love. . . . Love is the highest form of slavery." [9]

Dr. Ashley Montagu agrees: "What man wants is that

positive freedom which follows the pattern of his life as an infant within the family—dependent security, the feeling that one is a part of a group, accepted, wanted, loved and loving." [10]

Essentially, marriage is a matter of faith. A successful marriage, therefore, is a triumph of faith. What a magnificent thought for a fortieth, a fiftieth, or a sixtieth anniversary!

The sonnet Dr. Edward L. Christie wrote "For Margaret" sums up the deep feelings of a married lover who is certain his wedding band is for keeps:

I love to read the lines upon your face
Which bear a message no one else can know:
The laughter of two decades, light on snow
And mountain lake, the ludicrous grimace
That judges life with charitable grace;
The deeper lines engraved by secret woe,
Bereavement, heartaches, bravely borne through slow
Progress of time that leads us to this place.
This is a contour map where I may read
With reverence your soul's geography—
The heights, the depths, stark valleys of our need,
The luminous peaks of love's bright ecstasy.
The lines become more lovely with the years—
Our mutuality of fun and fears. [11]

14

ILLNESS WITHOUT
PANIC IS POSSIBLE

We never know how we are going to react to anything unpleasant until it hits us, and this is very true of illness—which nobody wants and everybody gets.

To some people almost any illness is reason for despair. Such people seem incapable of accepting anything more serious than a common cold without trumpeting that they may be nigh unto death. For such pessimists, the flu is the first stage of pneumonia. An after-dinner pain is prelude to acute indigestion. A cough is an authentic symptom of tuberculosis. A scratch is a sure forerunner of blood poisoning. A lump has to mean cancer. An energtic heartthrob is warning of sudden death by heart failure.

This is nonsense, of course. All of us should know that how we feel about our health has much to do with maintaining a state of health. People who engage in foolish worry about health matters may find that they have pushed themselves into an emotionally induced illness that a happy outlook could have avoided.

A young woman became seriously overweight and was advised to lose considerable weight—which she did by months of will power applied to a drastic diet. Then the happy day: The reducing goal was reached. Happy? No, for she had read that loss of weight can be a cancer symptom, and she promptly went into a depression until extensive (and expensive) tests proved that the weight loss meant only that she had succeeded in doing what the physician had recommended. In the meantime, insomnia and tension headaches had developed because of worry.

Why some people go into virtual panic when there is even a minor threat to their health would involve a careful individual study; generalizations would be useless. Perhaps there will always be individuals like the brilliant John Stuart Mill, who as a boy planned suicide because he was obsessed with the thought that some day all possible combinations of musical notes would be exhausted and further composition would be impossible.

Mill's pessimism was not basically different from that of the member of an audience who thought he heard a speaker say, "I calculate that the end of the world will come in 17 million years."

"How many years did you say?" the listener demanded.

"217—," the speaker began.

"What a relief!" sighed the questioner. "I thought you said 17 million years."

There is an opposite to the person who panics at the thought of illness or less-than-perfect health. He is the person who thrives on illness and more or less secretly hopes it will last a long time.

Usually such a person lives alone or feels alone, needs someone to talk with, and even more needs to be assured that other folks care. One way to determine whether anyone really cares is to become ill and let the news be widely spread. This is a rather desperate S.O.S. in search of affection, but it is much more likely to produce results than an appearance of self-sufficiency.

The problem with such a technique for arousing sympathy is that if overplayed or posed just once, the appeal is lost forever. Thereafter talk about heart, liver, stomach, or nerves is likely to be regarded as so much hypochondriac chatter to be endured if necessary, but avoided if possible.

There is a mature attitude toward illness that avoids both of the foolish extremes just described. It is best developed as far as possible in days of health. It begins with this policy:

Stay healthy if you can. Poor health is not necessarily the result of abusing the body, but physical abuse is responsible for a shocking percentage of illness.

Any physician will agree that no amount of precaution or prevention can guarantee perfect health. But any physician will also tell you that you can break your health by breaking the laws of health.

By now every smoker knows the truth about cigarettes and health. Smoking a pack a day shortens an average life about seven years.[1] Each cigarette smoked cuts eight to ten minutes from a life span.[2] We know that cigarettes not only cause lung cancer but heart disease, chronic bronchitis, emphysema, and even loss of teeth.[3]

Consumers' Research, with these blunt words, refused a request to test cigarettes: "If CR were to test and rate smoking products, we could not fail to list all cigarettes as *not recommended* for persons who desire to live as long as may be reasonably possible and remain free from lung cancer and heart disease."[4]

Americans need to be reminded also that alcoholism ranks with heart disease, cancer, and mental illness as one of the nation's four major health problems. So pervasive is the use of beverage alcohol that, until we notice the crash of a social drinker into the near-helpless depths of alcoholism, many of us ignore plain warnings and hazards.

The possibility of alcoholism is not so remote as is generally supposed. Authorities once believed that one of every fifteen social drinkers is destined to become an alcoholic; more recently experts are inclined to the belief that the ratio may be even more unfavorable to the social drinker. For the unlucky *one*, the process takes from seven to seventeen years. Which one of the fifteen or so casual drinkers will need the ministry of Alcoholics Anonymous cannot be determined in advance, a fact that makes the drinking of alcohol a form of Russian roulette.

The positive way to consider health is to determine to stay healthy as long as one possibly can. When illness comes, despite the implementation of this determination with knowledge and grit, there is only one thing for a person to do: *Go about recovering if possible.*

Americans should remember the examples left us by the struggle for health of both Roosevelts who became presidents of the United States and whose battles are a lasting challenge to the afflicted.

As a child Theodore Roosevelt suffered from asthma and was never strong enough to attend a public school. His eyes were so weak he could not read more than a few minutes at a time. Until "Teddy" Roosevelt was in his twenties, he went for months without relief from headaches. The heroic story of how he set aside all other plans in order to fight for health, how he won the battle, how he became one of the most vigorous men ever to live in the White House, is recommended reading for Americans of all ages.

The story of the other Roosevelt, the one who was four times elected to the presidency, is an even more dramatic narrative. Stricken with paralytic polio after a sensational beginning on the national political scene, "F.D.R." toughened both mind and body for a continuation of his career. The drama of the president who lived in a wheelchair in private and stood with the aid of steel braces in public, the paralyzed president who successfully led his nation through the worst economic disaster and the most serious war in its history, puts to shame every person who ever thought of giving up without a battle against disease or physical handicap.

Even when a person has done all he knows to do to stay healthy, he may fall prey to infection, to a virus, to an inherited family weakness—to something. He will then do everything he and his medical advisers know to do in order to recover as completely and as rapidly as possible.

But he may learn he is not likely to recover. He may have a chronic condition he must live with the rest of his life, a condition that may or may not threaten his longevity. He may have a more serious problem indicating a real and immediate struggle for life.

What then? The man or woman with a chronic disease soon discovers that he has a lot of company. Two out of five people over the age of sixty and more than five of six persons sixty-five or over are going about their lives with the knowledge that they no longer enjoy the clean bill of health their doctors were once so pleased to give them.[5] Many who are much younger face the reality that the days of routine physical examinations are over, and that constant medical observation and treatment will be the rule from now on.

Whether the handicap of disease, or a physical disability such as blindness or lameness, comes at six or sixty, the human response has to be the same: Go about recovering, if possible; if complete recovery is not possible, *make the best of it*.

When I was a boy, the gospel hymns of Fanny Crosby were exceedingly popular in most Protestant churches. We sang them with gusto, for they were songs born of a happy faith. Not until later did I learn that because of blundering treatment, Fanny Crosby was blinded at the age of six weeks. Her eight thousand hymns were created by a brave little woman who never saw sunshine. From the darkness of this woman's lifelong blindness came "Blessed Assurance" and "There Is Sunshine in My Soul" to cheer and strengthen millions around the world. She made the best of it!

And so did William Ernest Henley, the English boy who at the age of twelve suffered the amputation of a leg because of bone disease. In a strange city twelve years later, facing the possibility of losing his *other* leg, young Henley wrote "Invictus," which means "Unconquered." He began his poem with these words:

> Out of the night that covers me,
> 　Black as the Pit from pole to pole,
> I thank whatever gods may be
> 　For my unconquerable soul.

Henley made the best of it!

For the religious person, courage is more than Stoicism, the philosophic prop for endurance. He knows that spiritual opportunity comes with suffering. While he does not welcome the suffering, he welcomes the opportunity to grow in patience and unselfishness. These are not virtues that thrive ordinarily under cloudless skies.

The Christian recalls the greeting of Jesus to the paralytic man in Matthew 9:2—"Son, be of good cheer," as the King James Version has it, or "Take heart, my son," as it was translated for the Revised Standard Version. The good cheer of the suffering Christian is deeply rooted in his belief that Love is at the heart of things. Suffering there is, yes; but Love is the motivation and the reward of life.

15

BEREAVEMENT
CAN BE SURMOUNTED

When I was first given the opportunity to introduce college students to the poems of Tennyson, I wondered how I should prepare them for "In Memoriam A. H. H." and other expressions of grief such as the moving poem that contains these lines:

> But O for the touch of a vanish'd hand,
> And the sound of a voice that is still![1]

My presumption was that a class of students in their late teens and early twenties would be largely unacquainted with sorrow and grief.

How wrong I was! A girl told about the shock of her elder brother's death in a plane crash. A boy related the horror of a Christmas Eve when his sister died in a flaming automobile wreck. More students than I would have guessed had already lost one of their parents, and quite a number had been present at the death of a grandfather or grandmother.

"In the midst of life we are in death," reads the graveside service. It is a truth we are not long permitted to forget.

From childhood, therefore, human beings should grow accustomed to the cycle of life—birth–death, birth–death —which has always been and always will be. The possibility that someone in our closest circle of family and friends may be taken from us at any age, at any time, is a fact we have to accept regardless of how happy the present circumstances may be.

Acceptance of this possibility is the basis of the mammoth life insurance business as well as the basis for countless arrangements, legal and otherwise, that men make in anticipation of the undated inevitable. All this is simple realism, not morbidity.

Olivia de Havilland tells about a philosophic gardener of Spanish descent who was fond of quoting this line from *Don Quixote*: "A man prepared has half fought the battle." When Miss de Havilland was about to graduate from high school, she was extremely happy with the expectation that at the commencement exercises she would be announced as the salutatorian. But it was not so; she was third, not second, in the class. And she was heartbroken.

"You did not prepare yourself," José observed. "*It was possible*, and whatever is possible we must try to be ready to meet. *Sea preparada siempre!*" [2]

But the worst possibilities are very hard to prepare for. One day you have a son; the next day you do not. One day you have a husband; the next day he is gone. In theory these were possibilities all along, but stark reality is altogether different.

A woman in her fifties whose husband had died after a short illness sought a clergyman's advice. She was not a particularly religious woman, and she said she did not know how to start a prayer. "Then write God a letter," the minister suggested.

"Dear God," she wrote, "life has dealt me a very bad

hand. Please show me which card to lead. Sincerely," and she signed her name.

When bereavement strikes, either with a pounce or a crawl, what does a person do—what *can* he do in the face of irreversible reality?

1. **He can try to understand that he has suffered a severe emotional wound, the healing of which must take time.** He has been hurt, as he would have been hurt physically if he had fallen down the stairs or been struck by an automobile. The hurt is real, and he should expect to suffer and to cry.

And there should be no apology for tears. All of the customary ways by which suffering people express grief are ways intended by the Creator to cushion and finally heal emotional wounds.

But grief, though normal and helpful, must not be abnormally prolonged if life is to return to paths of stability and usefulness.

Tennyson described the first Christmas after the death of his friend Arthur Henry Hallam in these agonizing words:

> This year I slept and woke with pain,
> I almost wish'd no more to wake,
> And that my hold on life would break
> Before I heard those bells again.[3]

The second Christmas after the death of his close friend, Tennyson pondered, somewhat bewilderedly:

> Who show'd a token of distress?
> No single tear, no mark of pain:
> O sorrow, then can sorrow wane?
> O grief, can grief be changed to less?[4]

Later, fully recovered from his deep emotional wound, Tennyson wrote the following lines.

My pulses therefore beat again
   For other friends that once I met;
   Nor can it suit me to forget
The mighty hopes that make us men.[5]

I remember with pride the conduct of my mother during the three days between Father's death and his burial. Mother and Dad had been the closest of companions for nearly forty years, and Mother had not quite reached her sixtieth birthday when the separation occurred. She refused a sedative, but she spent much of the time before the funeral service half-reclining and resting in bed.

There in the bedroom she met her friends and talked about the wonderful years she had enjoyed with the man who was her girlhood choice. Holding the family album and a collection of snapshots in her hands, she turned the pages lovingly, breaking into tears now and then but also, with almost equal frequency, breaking into smiles and quiet laughter. It had been a good life together, and she was thankful.

Mother probably never read a book about problem-solving or emotional therapy. But with the instinctive common sense of a well-adjusted personality that had already experienced life in both its dark and light moods, she was prepared for the worst possibility of all. For this lesson—and many others—I thank her.

How different was the reaction of another mother when the life of one of her three children was taken by a hit-and-run driver. In her case a physician was needed not only once but many times in the years that followed the tragedy. Sedatives were prescribed at first, but anxiety soon developed that called for a steady treatment of tranquilizers. Because the mother's wild grief persisted, affecting her health and her relations with the rest of the family, the father suggested that they sell the home and move to another location.

Moving was not the solution. In the new home the mother developed the habit of spending her afternoons washing and ironing the clothing of the daughter who had died more than a year earlier. Grief, nourished to the exclusion of normal interests and responsibilities, finally resulted in serious mental illness.

"There is a time to weep, and a time to laugh; a time to mourn, and a time to dance" wrote the author of Ecclesiastes (3:4). Under normal circumstances the "time to weep" is limited not only by the expectations of friends and relatives but by the swift passing of time. The Bible records the fact that Abraham, Jacob, and David all wept publicly, but only while the "time to weep" lasted.

Rabbinic literature of Judaism divided the time of mourning into definite periods. "The first three days are given to weeping and lamentation. The deceased is eulogized up to the seventh day, the mourner keeping within the house. The somber garb of mourning is worn up to the thirtieth day, and personal adornment is neglected." [6] This prescribed progression from the depths of fresh grief to the paths of normal living, though devised long before the days of psychiatrists and psychologists, is as sound today as it was a thousand years ago.

Besides attempting valiantly to believe that the intensity of new grief will diminish, what can a man or woman do if bereavement strikes?

2. Get busy. Two days after fire destroyed a house, a reporter saw the man of the house sorting hot bricks that once formed his home. "I'm figuring out how soon these bricks will be cool enough for me to start rebuilding," was his explanation.

Get busy! There is no better advice for anyone smarting

from emotional injury. The alternative is to mope around indefinitely, expecting only barren years ahead, feeling sorry for oneself, alienating those who are ready to extend a welcome back to the circle of life and activity.

There is food for thought in Dr. John Schindler's discovery: "The group in my part of the country who have emotionally induced illness least often are the farmers' wives with big families who, in addition to their housework, also help out on the farm. . . . They are too busy taking care of other people to think of themselves." [7]

3. **Seek companionship.** The world is full of people who know what bereavement means. "Thy fate is the common fate of all," as Longfellow expressed it.

Sometime after the evacuation of Dunkirk early in World War II, a friend asked a British soldier about his experience on the beach. "What did it feel like, out there on that beach in Dunkirk, with the sea in front of you, the German army back of you, and the German bombers over you?"

His reply: "It was a strange feeling I had. I felt that every man on the beach was my brother." [8]

There is indeed among the family of mankind a brotherhood of suffering. In that brotherhood is healing, understanding, and friendship.

4. **Live the faith.** Confiding to his diary on September 12, 1893, Robert Louis Stevenson wrote of his South Pacific journey in search of health: "I have written in bed, and written out of bed, written in hemorrhages, written in sickness, written when my head swam from weakness. . . . The battle goes on. *But I was made for a contest.*" [9]

This is another way of saying that God does not expect man to carry heavier burdens than he was created to carry. Capacity to suffer and endure varies from person to person, to be sure, and for most people there is a breaking point. A man who lives his faith, however, is not likely to discover whether he has a breaking point.

An essential part of this faith is the belief that *life is worth living*. Many people, alas, are hit so violently by experiences in life that they come to doubt this basic condition for stability and survival. When someone asked Eugene O'Neill why he never wrote about happy people, he answered, "I'll write about happiness if I ever happen to meet up with that luxury. . . . " But later he declared, "I'm tickled to death with life. I wouldn't go out and miss the rest of the play for anything." [10] Nor would anyone in his right mind. Happiness is a habit worthy of cultivation.

The belief that *the soul of man does not die with the body* is also a basic ingredient of faith. Men have various understandings of this faith, but it is impossible to affirm the spiritual nature of the universe and to accept a Creative Mind and Soul without believing that the souls of men come from the Divine and that they "dwell in the house of the Lord for ever."

PART IV

The Unfolding of Happiness

16

YOUTH IS
FOR PROMISE

"Youth is not a time of life—it is a state of mind . . . it is a freshness of the deep springs of life." Thus begins a statement that has hung in my study since I became a college president at the age of thirty, many years ago. I believed it then. I believe its essential truth now.

To discuss the paradox of happiness as it relates to youth requires an understanding regarding the term "youth." Adolescence, the period of sexual awakening and movement toward independence, is normally associated with the teens—thirteen through nineteen. Adolescence through early adulthood—roughly thirteen to twenty-two—is the period when decisions are made that determine nearly everything for the middle and later years. The period of youth is life——vigorous, hopeful, beautiful life for most —but not yet life in fulfillment.

The problem society has in determining when adolescence ends and early adulthood begins is the source of continuous difficulties in school, college, home, courts, and throughout our culture generally. Confusion starts when parenthood becomes possible early in adolescence. Confusion is compounded whenever authority figures in the adult world act as if capability of parenthood proves emotional and value-based maturity of the type associated with true adulthood.

The fact is, of course, that the usual adolescent gives only the illusion of adulthood. In height, weight, and physical strength, the adolescent is often equal to or superior to the adult; but the resemblance ends there.

Not long ago I went three times a week from a class of college freshmen and sophomores to a class of juniors and seniors. The difference between the two classes was the difference between adolescence and young adulthood. The earlier class manifested many attributes of high-school students; the later class contained several who would have been at home in a graduate class. Yet Dr. H. Waldo Bird, former professor of psychiatry at St. Louis University, confirms the common impression that "most young adults do not possess fully matured personalities." [1]

Until young adults reach the fully matured stage of adulthood (and some will never arrive), most of them are not aware of their halfway state and consequently believe they have exchanged adolescence for adulthood. Noteworthy, therefore, is an editorial written by a college sophomore following a destructive fraternity bid festival on his campus. "The administration," the young editor wrote, "has got to change its policy of taking for granted all students are mature enough to make unquestioned judgments in everything they do. Obviously not all are mature and responsible citizens of this campus. Thus, disciplinary rules and action *have* to be enforced." [2] (Student editors are not always this perceptive or frank in telling their peers unpleasant truths about themselves.)

The relationship of young people, especially adolescents, to authority—policeman, parent, teacher, school or college administrator—is paradoxical. On the surface the demand of youth is for total freedom from authority; yet the authority who surrenders his authority forfeits the respect of those who demand it.

"No matter how long adolescents argue, no matter how loudly they accuse adults of lack of feeling, interest, and understanding," says Dr. Robert J. McAllister, psychiatrist, "they do want someone to be strong and to tell them where the line must be drawn. . . . It frightens them when there are no external controls." [3]

A thoughtful American educator, Dr. John R. Silber, now president of Boston University, predicted: "In the year 2000 we may have, and I believe we shall have, some of the most repressed and repressive grandchildren that the world has ever seen. A generation that has suffered for more than twenty years in the wilderness of experimentation will clamp the rules down again. But this time the rules won't be enforced because of tradition; they will be enforced because of the hard-won and dearly bought experience of the parental generation now in college." [4]

None of this is to say that adults should dictate and that youth should keep silent while toeing the mark. Dialogue is essential. (A father, asked whether his son was one of the alienated, answered, "I don't know. We never talk to each other.")

A wise adult will regard a certain amount of conflict with his children or his students as inevitable and even desirable. No one really grows up without questioning the establishment, and no one is qualified to become the establishment without first questioning its roots. One of the lessons of history cited by Will and Ariel Durant following completion of their monumental ten-volume work is this: "It is good that the old should resist the young, and that the young should prod the old; out of this tension comes a tensile strength, a stimulated development, a secret and basic unity and movement of the whole." [5]

Despite the dialogue forced by campus unrest and youth

protests in the sixties, there are indications that youth power is as sporadic and uncertain as before. The U.S. Census Bureau, for example, reports that in the 1972 presidential election only 48 percent of the newly enfranchised voters aged 18 to 20 cast ballots—in contrast to 68 percent of voters in the 65-to-74 age group. In the Congressional election of 1974 only 21 percent of the 18-to-20 age group voted compared with 58 percent of the 55-to-64 group.

Those students who believed they should run the colleges and universities, presumably because they are the largest groups on the campuses, are now having second thoughts about their time, their interest, and their qualifications.

(At a student government meeting, a committee chairman reported, "The Committee on Campus Apathy has no report. Only three of the fifteen members showed up for the meeting.")

The notion that a democracy of equals exists either in a home or on a campus is giving way to recognition of inequality of information, experience, wisdom. The result is neither elitism nor authoritarianism. It is a move toward Jefferson's dream of an aristocracy of achievement arising out of a democracy of opportunity.

The chief worry of concerned parents, teachers, and administrators is that some kind of disaster may occur that would handicap a young person in striving toward his potential. The disaster could be physical, but it could be moral, spiritual, artistic, or intellectual.

The years of youth are fleeting, like all years, and those things that should be accomplished at the outset of life ordinarily have to be dealt with then or never. The "hell of the irrevocable" is Josiah Royce's description of this inescapable fact. Paul Laurence Dunbar described it this way:

> Slight was the thing I bought,
> Small was the debt I thought,

Poor was the loan at best—
God! but the interest! [6]

Yale's chaplain, the Reverend William Sloane Coffin, Jr., says that in 1958 he used to say to a senior with whom he had become well acquainted, "You're a nice guy, Jeb, but not yet a good man. You have lots of charm but little inner strength. And if you don't stand for something you're apt to fall for anything." [7]

Sixteen years later that senior, Jeb Stuart Magruder, a confessed felon caught in the Watergate web, stood before a federal judge and said, "I know what I have done, and your honor knows what I have done. . . . Somewhere between my ambition and my ideals, I lost my ethical compass." [8]

How can young people avoid the mistakes that eventually ruin their careers and their lives? Advice from older, more experienced people seems the logical means of avoiding trouble, but advice seldom works. "Has any man ever attained inner harmony by pondering the experience of others? Not since the world began! He must pass through the fire." Thus spoke an anonymous seer.

If a youth is not to be destroyed by avoidable experience, he must build up resistance to ignorance, folly, and sin —like the production of antibodies—by developing as rapidly as possible a body of *faith*—commitment to values, and *practice*—commitment to ethical choice. This is a big order for an adolescent or even an adult, but many young people have the insight and moral stamina to do just that. They are the young who "stand on their own two feet" and become in later years the chief support of a civilized society.

The use or nonuse of marijuana continues to be a live issue for the young, not only in urban centers but in many remote rural areas. Most parents and teachers have heard the explanation for its widespread use: sociability, pleasure, harmlessness. A coed pot smoker said in one of my classes, "Marijuana never hurt anybody, and it should be legalized. So far as the heart is concerned, marijuana excites the heart less than sex—which everybody knows is harmless."

Use of heroin, cocaine, LSD, it is agreed, is one thing; marijuana quite another. But whether the latter usually leads to the former is not a matter of agreement. As results are obtained from long-term studies of marijuana use, however, it is beginning to appear that the harmless drug is not so harmless as many have supposed.

A Columbia University research group, for example, reports direct evidence of cellular damage to habitual pot smokers. Weekly smoking of pot or hashish for at least a year, they discovered, seriously weakened the body's defenses against disease. White blood cells, the Columbia researchers found, reproduced 40 percent less in pot smokers than in nonsmokers.[9]

Dr. Dana L. Farnsworth, former director of Harvard University's Health Services, has this answer to those who believe marijuana is harmless: "They have not seen the tragic alterations of young lives or the frequent escalation to more dangerous drugs with which the physician in a college health service is familiar. Marijuana does not *necessarily* lead to stronger drugs, but it can and does."[10]

In 1967 the chief psychiatrist in the Student Health Center of the University of California, at Berkeley, D. Harvey Powelson, M.D., told the student newspaper: "There is no evidence that marijuana does anything except make people feel good." Seven years later, however, after counseling two hundred students with problems resulting from marijuana use, Dr. Powelson announced, "I now believe that marijuana is the most dangerous drug we have to contend with today for these reasons: *Its early use is beguiling.* Pot smokers are so enraptured by the *illusion* of warm feelings that they are unable to sense the deterioration of their own mental and physiological processes. *Its continued use leads to delusional thinking.* And along with the delusions comes the strong need to seduce others into using drugs. I have rarely seen a regular marijuana user who didn't actively attempt to influence friends to use the drug." [11]

For twenty years there has been growing evidence that another kind of smoking—cigarette smoking—is so dangerous as to be a real threat to the life of every habitual smoker. By 1954 the National Cancer Conference and the Public Health Cancer Association were pointing out the close connection between cigarette smoking and lung cancer. On January 11, 1964, a 387-page document issued by the surgeon general of the U.S. Public Health Service formally indicted cigarette smoking as a major hazard to life and health.

Public health officials are inclined to believe that without the surgeon general's report and the further scientific studies that have followed, 75 million people in this country would be cigarette smokers today instead of the estimated 52 million. But the surgeon general of 1964 lamented in 1974: "I'm most discouraged by our lack of success with youth. . . . They're starting at earlier ages and there's been a dramatic increase in the percentage of girls who smoke." [12]

Why? Is the cigarette for some young people an alternative for drugs or alcohol? Is cigarette smoking a symbol of adulthood? Is it an imitation of parents, teachers, coaches, even pastors?

Whatever the explanation, the promise of uncounted young people will be cut short unless they somehow learn the truth about cigarettes and act accordingly. The surgeon general's lengthy indictment of 1964, never seriously contradicted, accused cigarette smoking of being the main cause of lung cancer and chronic bronchitis and a contributing cause of cancer of the larynx, bladder, and esophagus; as well as increasing the risk of heart disease, peptic ulcers, cirrhosis of the liver, and smallness of babies at birth.

According to the *New York Times*, the list of health hazards now directly associated with cigarette smoking has been broadened to include cancer of the mouth, pharynx, pancreas and kidney, atherosclerosis and several vascular diseases, gum disease, emphysema, and heart disease. In the same article, Great Britain's chief medical officer, Sir George Godber, says that cigarettes are responsible for nine in ten lung cancer deaths, three in four chronic bronchitis deaths, and one in four deaths from heart disease.[13] The U.S. Public Health Service summarizes: "The risk of death from all causes is 70 percent higher for cigarette smokers than for non-smokers."

In God's name, then, why does anyone allow himself to become dependent on a smelly pollutant of nicotine and tar unless he wants premature death—possibly slow and painful at that? The promise of youth! How fragile it becomes in the presence of ignorance, indifference, and irresponsibility.

It was a scientist, not an intentional killjoy, who called alcoholism "a much more dangerous addiction than all of the other drug addictions put together."[14] But how are parents, teachers, and ministers to protect a new generation from alcoholism when beverage alcohol has become the center of virtually every social occasion and when nondrinkers (except medical dropouts and members of Alcoholics Anonymous, of course) are regarded as freaks? And how can inexperienced young people protect themselves when society regards alcohol as no more hazardous than milk?

The answers to these questions are not easy. We have to understand that of the 95 million Americans who are now consuming more alcohol per capita than at any previous time in our history, about *one in ten* (according to HEW's National Institute on Alcohol Abuse and Alcoholism) is either an alcoholic or a problem drinker, i.e., a person whose drinking is causing real trouble for himself and for society.[15]

Surely no one ever took his first alcoholic drink with the hope or expectation of becoming an alcoholic or a problem drinker. There is clearly, then, an insidious aspect to the use of alcoholic beverages that the beginning or purely social drinker is often not in a position to recognize. "If you need a drink to be social," reads an NIAAA ad, "that's not social drinking." Of course not, but when "need" has become the cause of drinking, the stage of real trouble has been reached.

The best dean of students I know, Dr. Joseph A. Bartell, says that college students in trouble because of alcoholic excesses nearly always maintain that they had only "a couple o' beers." He wonders whether they lose count after the first two beers.[16] *I* wonder whether they know that 30 to 40 percent of all alcoholics, according to an experienced counselor, have seldom consumed anything alcoholic except beer, the so-called drink of moderation. They are victims, says Alex Majewski, of the myth that only hard liquor can cause alcoholism.[17]

A few people, about 10 percent of all alcoholics, are what Marty Mann, founder of the National Council on Alcoholism, calls "instant alcoholics." They do not require the period of years needed by most potential alcoholics to reach the point of no return.[18]

For young people whose promise is not to be violated by excessive alcohol consumption, two factors are most important: parental example and early, thorough, sincere education in the truth about alcohol. Education is, obviously, the best way to prepare teen-agers to deal with the lure of both cigarettes and drugs (including alcohol).

The difficulty, despite the desperate need, is to find teachers in the home, school, and church sufficiently independent to risk charges of fanaticism by teaching sound scientific information essential to young life in this permissive age. Bans are futile. The "kids" will make their own decisions.

But they can be taught to operate the human organism by the book and not to expect health and stamina to result from abuse. People who enjoy at least average genetic inheritance and who supply their bodies with proper food, rest, exercise, and enthusiasm, will discover that they were created marvelously complete. They will not need alcohol to have fun, drugs to obtain peace of mind, caffeine to supply energy, or nicotine to relieve boredom.

Today's generation of young people have been given the freedom some of them sought. Guidelines of the past have been discarded generally, and nothing has been provided in their place. Until recently, colleges and universities believed that education of the "whole man" involved a clear position on those basic moralities that have marked civilized man. Pushed by a tidal wave of moral permissiveness and hoping to quell student unrest by surrender of all campus rules, many if not most of our institutions of higher education have now abandoned objectives intended to influence young life in the direction of socially accepted morality.

The ultimate in contemporary university "discipline" was suggested by a *Playboy* cartoon showing a residence hall director speaking to a voluptuous coed whose room was visited by all sorts and conditions of young men: "Yes," the director said, "you can do your own thing here, but you're not supposed to charge for it."

College administrators excuse their open-dorm policies by explaining that residence hall rooms are merely substitutes for motels and automobiles, and that students who intend to have sexual intercourse will do so regardless of anything the institution may do. Besides, there is a laughable tendency to claim that sex is of little interest to couples secure behind closed doors.

"You don't date at ————," says an honest senior girl. "You have a series of pseudo-marriages."

Another girl is sorry she could not have gone to college a few years earlier "when there were fewer things to decide. You didn't have to decide you didn't want to go to bed with a guy on the first date." [19]

University health services are adapting to new student problems by providing contraceptives, by adding gynecologists to the staff, by including vasectomies in the list of surgical services, by abortion referral service, by increased attention to venereal disease, and even by sex therapy of the Masters and Johnson type. [20]

But the question persists: Is everybody happy? Not so, according to Dr. Ernest Shaw, former campus psychiatrist at Vassar: "Students can't handle the lack of boundaries. They're looking for more control." [21]

A student at Michigan State says: "I was all for coed living at first. It was instant freedom. The trouble is that as a freshman coming in, you didn't quite know how to handle it. . . . You could have your girl friend in every night in complete privacy. . . . Did you ever try studying with a girl in your bedroom?" [22]

College and university counselors are dealing with many young women who are in depression from the shock of abandonment. In hope and faith, perhaps in love, they gave themselves to an eager sexual partner who after a period of "marriage" decided to move on to another room and another partner. "Sex is a game" or "sex is just like a good meal" is the rationale of men (or women) who do not require even tentative faithfulness as justification for bed-hopping.

Vassar freshmen heard Dr. Mary Calderone challenge "the game" or "the good meal" concept of sex by sound psychological reasoning: "There is no possibility of having sexual intercourse without meshing a part of your non-physical self. Sex is such a definite experience that a part of each of you remains forever a part of the other." [23]

And Rollo May, the writer-psychiatrist, concludes: "What we did not see in our short-sighted liberalism in sex was that throwing the individual into an unbounded and empty sea of free choice does not in itself give freedom, but is more apt to increase inner conflict. . . . So much sex and so little meaning or even fun in it!" [24]

"Youth Is for Promise" is not intended to be a chapter of despair. I know too many young people too well to think that most of them will not recognize the hazards involved in growing to maturity in an environment deficient in principles and moral boundaries. Some of them, in high school and in college, are amazingly mature already. I have told friends of my age that when I go into a classroom, I look at students as if I were blind; their attire and their hair are insignificant compared with their ideals, their insights, their ambitions. When I realize the maturity of many young men and women of my acquaintance, I take heart, for I am confident they will overcome.

The promise of youth depends upon basic choices made by young people in their teens and early twenties. They decide how much formal education or training their abilities and aspirations call for. They decide at least the general direction of their lives with respect to the use of time and energy. They choose, in most cases, a partner for the road ahead. And they decide what is important in life, what values they will prize and defend, what faith they will cherish until life ends.

Knowing how the range of choice narrows as life moves on, older people—parents, grandparents, friends, neighbors, teachers, pastors—are apt to be fearful of the ability of the young to make safe decisions. Some of these young people, alas, will make disastrously wrong decisions from which they will never fully recover. But one generation cannot live life for another. The generation ahead can only beckon and teach—and hope and pray.

17

MIDDLE AGE
IS FOR ACHIEVEMENT

Youth is a silly, vapid state;
Old age with fears and ills is rife;
This simple boon I beg of Fate—
A thousand years of Middle Life! [1]

However wonderful the experience of youth may be, and
however satisfying the retirement years may prove, in retro-
spect the middle years are almost always seen as the apex
of life—the part of life for which youth was a preparation
and old age an exercise in remembrance and thankfulness.

No wonder, then, that Carolyn Wells wished for a thousand years of middle age. William Saroyan must have had
something of the same thought when he divided life into
three unequal stages: "Be. Beget. Begone."

The boundaries of middle age will never be agreed upon
simply because people are reluctant to accept either the
end of youth or the onset of age. "The only time you really
live fully," says a character in *Anthony Adverse*, "is from
thirty to sixty." [2] This, of course, is a gross and largely
false simplification, but its origin is understandable.

Not long ago sixty was thought to be a safe, arbitrary

dividing point between middle age and old age. Sex was supposed to end about that time, and sixty-five was considered the upper age limit for anyone to be employed. To knowledgeable people all this is nonsense.

Forty has long been termed the old age of youth and the youth of old age, but this designation is superficial and omits the major segment of life. To youthful radicals of the sixties, thirty was the proper termination of youth. Since the average American has lived half of his life when he is around thirty-five, middle age can honestly be said to begin at thirty.

From the standpoint of typical life patterns, middle age —from youthful to advanced—extends a long, fruitful forty years from thirty to seventy. During these years, as Grandma Moses said, "Time goes on just the same. You don't have to watch it. You just use it."

When I was in my thirties, an insurance salesman showed me a chart of human life detailing its various periods. The decade between thirty and forty, I well remember, was labeled "The Golden Years." This I pondered but was not old enough to understand.

Now I do understand. Though I have found every decade of life golden in its pleasures, challenges, and opportunities, I see that the thirties offer uniquely the reward of mature life firmly established but yet capable of change and advancement; of family life complete with healthy parents, growing children, and adoring, still-active grandparents; and of fresh dependence on a faith and a philosophy newly but finally achieved.

It is when the forties and fifties are reached that middle age frequently presents problems, some of them frightfully serious. These are the years, as someone said, of bifocals, bridges, bulges, and baldness. But these are not the real problems. A woman revealed the chief danger of maturity when she confessed to E. Stanley Jones, "I'm about to jell into the kind of person I don't want to be."

Midway through middle age, years of work and achievement, life levels off. We no longer wonder what our lives are going to be like. We know that life is going to be what it is: *this is it!*

And this can be a shock. Unless the job, the marriage, the house, the neighbors, the in-laws, the boss, the community are near-perfect, the dread of the future can grow and embitter. In "Ashes of Life" Edna St. Vincent Millay describes this frustration with icy precision:

> And life goes on forever like the gnawing of a mouse,
>   And tomorrow and tomorrow and tomorrow and
>   tomorrow
> There's this little street and this little house.[3]

For the wife, life is not today's three meals, but tomorrow's and tomorrow's. For the jobholder, life is not today's responsibilities and annoyances, but every day's, for years and years to come. For everyone on the *plateau* of life, the hazards of monotony are real and dangerous. As with a passenger on a jet flight, the time between the steep ascent and the gradual descent will be long and boring unless he finds ways to pass the time pleasantly.

For the man or woman who has achieved an adult pattern of living that serves the individual's basic needs, middle age presents no major problems. If he or she is reasonably content with the typical day's outlets for energy, talent, companionship, and love, one could wish that middle age would last not a thousand years but forever.

A patient asked a physician why he worked so hard and how he kept up the pace. His answer: "I never work. I enjoy what I do." The worker who is in the right job can blend his work and his play so that there is no wall between them. Another physician, Dr. Alfred C. Cantor, advises his patients, "Let your work become your hobby. It is merely a matter of attitude. If you learn to enjoy what you do, you will be full of pep and energy at the end of a busy day." [4]

"Do you hear the solemn ticking of the clock?" an evangelist asked as he put his hand on a sinner's shoulder. "And do you know what day it relentlessly brings nearer?" "Yes," replied the man, "pay day."

For people who stray into the wrong kind of work and stay too long, life is a dreary round of waiting for pay day. When I hear a person say, "I just have to get away," I think of Psalm 55:

> O that I had wings like a dove!
> I would fly away and be at rest (v. 6).

A perpetual yearning to fly away indicates faulty adjustment to one's chosen means of earning a living.

The longest vacation imaginable will do a worker no good if he comes back to a job he hates. I shudder when I think of a letter written to the financial columnist of a daily newspaper. It began: "I am 64. For 44 years I have worked hard in order to retire at 65 and enjoy life." Imagine planning to enjoy life *beginning* at age 65! The poor man wouldn't know how.

In my experience as a college administrator I came to know many colleagues whose energies and enthusiasms were renewed by their daily work. One was a cook whose sweetrolls fattened many a happy student. One was a janitor whose waxed floors reflected his pride of workmanship. One was a professor who joyfully spent forty years teaching from a wheelchair. Another was a dean who loved his work and believed everyone could learn to work in the same spirit.

Few happy middle-aged people I have known have been free from the usual elements of unhappiness—sickness, physical handicap, financial worries, family problems, disappointment, frustration. Henry Thoreau, observing the letdown that often comes to people midstream in life, wrote in his *Journal:* "The youth gets his materials together to build a bridge to the moon, or, perchance, a palace or temple on the earth, and, at length, the middle-aged man concludes to build a woodshed with them." [5]

The point: He builds *something!* He may not be a United States senator as once he dreamed, but he serves usefully as a member of the local board of education. She may not be interpreting Mozart with the Philharmonic at Lincoln Center, but she is introducing scores of young people from the neighborhood to the joys of playing the piano. And so on and so on.

The paradox of happiness in middle age is the acceptance of life, not as it was expected to be, but as it is and will likely continue to be.

One of my most valued friends at the outset of a career in college administration was Rabbi George B. Lieberman, orator, scholar, and trusted spiritual leader. He was obviously a young rabbi with a secure future.

Then one night, when Rabbi Lieberman was traveling by train around the famous Altoona horseshoe curve, a terrible accident occurred and he was trapped for hours in an upper berth while rescuers sought to reach the dead and the injured. As best he could, while waiting for release, he comforted his terrified companions. Nearly three years later, after long convalescence and persistent doubt that he could ever resume his calling, he made his way into his Canton pulpit, aided by steel braces on his back and legs, and began a sermon.

"What," he asked, "are life's most precious posses-sions?" He spoke of simple things, homely matters, things we take for granted like the air we breathe. He had learned a good deal since he had last stood in this pulpit. Most of all, he had found the secret of happiness. Happi-ness was to be found in self-acceptance, "to accept one-self amidst the sudden realization of irretrievable youth and the inescapable reality of growing old, to accept one-self with ambitions unrealized, success unattained, oppor-tunities muffed, regrets unhealed. . . ." [6]

This was not meant to be resignation or surrender but a resolute facing of reality. "Courage is fear that has said its prayers," a soldier testified. Margaret Bailey put it this way:

> God, give me sympathy and sense
> And help me keep my courage high.
> God, give me calm and confidence—
> And, please—a twinkle in my eye. [7]

Dr. Fosdick expressed concern about young Christians whose religion is expressed entirely in activism; "aggres-sive activists" he called them. "I never see people like that," he said one Sunday morning in Riverside Church, "without knowing what will come some day: soon or late it will inevitably come. . . : real sorrow, for example . . . serious failure . . . disappointment. We need the inner resources that make *endurance* possible." [8]

Charles A. Lindbergh knew that in attempting the first solo flight across the Atlantic he was risking his life. His attitude was: "A pilot has the right to choose his battle-field—that is the strategy of flight. But once the battlefield is attained, conflict should be welcomed, not avoided. If the pilot fears to test his skill with the elements, he has chosen the wrong profession." [9]

People in the middle years should know life well enough to expect conflict and to be prepared to test their skills against each new adversary. Total freedom from anxiety and tension they should neither expect nor desire.

"It's tough for doctors to deal realistically with people who . . . have the crazy idea that they should live a tension-free life," complains Dr. Edwin Roberts, New York psychiatrist.[10] "Anxiety," Freud told a patient, "is our lot as men."

For people who have not yet learned in middle age the art of self-acceptance, Max Ehrmann's advice is bitter medicine: "Take kindly the counsel of the years, gracefully surrendering the things of youth."[11] Perpetual youth is the really impossible dream. We can remain youthful in adaptability, in hopefulness, in cheerfulness, but we cannot stay young. Those who have such dreams should think about this truth: "You are young only once, but you can stay immature indefinitely."

A well-known American woman, who insists on being quoted anonymously, describes a basic immaturity in certain men and women obviously past the days of youth: "Millions of goods are sold and millions of hours are spent in pursuit of a youth which no longer exists and which cannot be recaptured. The result of this [is] . . . pathetic."

One of the dangers of middle age is futile rebellion against the years. Life is not a clock that can be moved either forward or backward; it is a steady, one-direction progression of the years. A fortune may be spent on cosmetics and plastic surgery, but in time we get old just the same.

Perhaps the chief danger of middle age is refusal to rebel against intellectual and spiritual decay. Formal education usually ends in the teens or early twenties. What lasting effects are evident in the forties? What evidence of increasing maturity, depth, understanding, or wisdom is shown after two or three decades have passed? If real education is what remains after the facts have been forgotten, what remains in the forties? If idealism is a characteristic of youth, the ultimate question is what ideals and what kind of character have remained and have been developed in middle life?

These matters should be the primary concern of men and women who live on the plateau stage of life. But are they? Dr. William H. Sheldon thinks not:

> The days of youth teem with fragments of living knowledge; with dawning philosophies; morning dreams; plans. But the human mind at forty is commonly vulgar, smug, deadened, and wastes its hours. Everywhere adult brains seem to resemble blighted trees that have died in the upper branches, but yet cling to a struggling green wisp of life about the lower trunk.[12]

People who at forty read what they read at eighteen, hear the same kind of music, admire the same works of art, specialize in the same amusements, rehash the same conversational subjects, have the same understanding of God and man, were either precocious at eighteen or are retarded now. The signs of life in human beings are deepening interests, wider horizons, more intensive knowledge, greater wisdom. If intellectual and spiritual growth and vitality continue until the late thirties, they will probably continue throughout life, having become habitual. But God pity the second half of life for the person who is a vegetable at forty!

Be warned that human vegetables—or at least adult children—are assumed to be the consumers when many television programs are planned, when a lot of radio shows are thrown together, often when newspaper space allocations are determined, when most movies are produced, and—I have noticed sorrowfully—when many radio sermons are preached.

A significant development in terms of opportunity for human growth in middle life is the widespread availability of college and university evening courses. Granted that an amazing number of these courses (especially those offered by community colleges) are nonintellectual and noncultural, opportunity will usually be found to enroll for courses that stretch the intellect and challenge the spirit. Such courses should be especially attractive for "plateau" people who recognize that they largely wasted their years in high school or college, having been too immature to profit by the education then set before them.

Closely related to intellectual decay is the spiritual rot that frequently occurs in middle age. When ideas disappear, ideals are apt to follow. Young people are not often materialistic in their values, but something sad can easily happen to one's values on the way to middle age. The big car, the big house, the big stock portfolio do not *prove* a reversal of spiritual priorities, but such possessions need to be evaluated seriously in the light of total life design. Is the Cadillac the end objective of living? Or is it an affordable bonus that follows education, books, flowers, music, art, charities, churches, and travel-to-learn?

I like Rabbi Joshua Liebman's approach to this dimension of life: "I will strive to achieve a mature attitude toward success which is ambition for growth and achievement . . . rather than acquisition." [13] It was this attitude that caused a husband and wife to stop worrying about their expensive silver service. It was the pride of their home. They had protected and babied it. But at length they saw the silliness of their constant concern. They printed a neat sign, which they put on the dining room table when they went to bed and when they left on vacations. The sign read: "Hello Burglar—the silver is in the chest on the right." They worried no more.

Spiritual decay resulting from humdrum living is usually the explanation for middle-aged people who "jump the track." Surely a middle-aged adulterer could not justify his conduct on the basis of ignorance or inexperience.

We must concede, to be sure, that emotions related to the sex drive are difficult to control unless they are meshed into a highly satisfactory living arrangement. Hamlet was probably naive, as young people usually are in these matters, when he informed his mother, "At your age the heyday of the blood is tame; it's humble, and waits upon the judgment." [14]

Judgment can fail, of course, and obviously has failed when a bank cashier elopes with a secretary and a bundle of the bank's cash. Judgment always tries to tell such a man that what he wants to do is morally and legally wrong and that he will be caught, convicted, sentenced—and disgraced. The mature walk into trouble with their eyes open. ("O my!" said the minister when he heard about the bank cashier's elopement and embezzlement, "Who'll teach his Sunday School class?")

It is as likely to be a church school teacher as anyone who falls into the pit of a middle-aged infatuation. In *The Screwtape Letters* C. S. Lewis contends: "The long, dull monotonous years of middle-aged prosperity or middle-aged adversity are excellent campaigning weather [for the Devil]." [15] "Died at thirty, buried at sixty" was G. B. Shaw's epitaph for the unthinking person of supposed maturity.

There is a sameness about plateau living, observers agree, that lack of contentment in married life and lack of enthusiasm about life generally may turn into wild and impulsive action. Remember King David, man of maturity, his battles won, his neat kingdom in order, who in an hour of boredom slipped and started an avalanche that nearly ruined his life.

It is not surprising that monogamy sometimes turns into monotony. But it need not be so. True lovers know the danger signs. They also know the need for deserved mutual respect and for shared experiences of the most intimate sort. "Make memories," a widow advises.

Let us repeat, in conclusion, what we all know: The middle years can be the muddle years or the happy years of work and achievement. Happiness comes and stays with those who find the meaning of life in living.

18

OLD AGE IS FOR
TESTING AND REWARD

This chapter is primarily for people who are young enough to undertake the most important project of their lives —education for old age.

If any old people (older people, pardon me!) are curious, let them read on; no one will interfere. But they should be warned that lamentations may follow.

"A negligent youth," wrote Anne Bradstreet, first poet of England's American colonies, "is usually attended by an ignorant middle age, and both by an empty old age." [1] Emptiness in old age does not occur overnight; it must be provided for by youthful and middle years of attention to interests that are destined to end with employment or with the life-style of middle age.

"One-track minds have nowhere to go after retirement has derailed them," explains that stimulating columnist, Sydney Harris. "Nobody can suddenly change at 65. . . . The development of the total personality must be an ongoing process, so that retirement from work does not mean retirement from life. . . ." [2]

But when retirement or death of one's life partner occurs, the patterns of decades are shattered. Let no one charge that older people have lost the capacity to adjust. Changes that follow bereavement or permanent loss of employment are as drastic as any that occur in a lifetime, and they are accompanied by emotions and sentiments developed over many years. Yet aging people usually *do* adjust to smaller incomes and homes, separation from colleagues and loved ones, decreasing vigor and status, change of time schedules, new social attitudes—and they even learn to resist the myth that older people are peculiar and generally useless.

It is idle, though, to expect that a large percentage of people will arrive at old age fully prepared intellectually and spiritually for life without employment, without the respect of earlier years, without a companion, and eventually *with* declining health and energy.

Simone de Beauvoir says that "if old age is not to be an absurd parody of our former life," we must "go on pursuing ends that give our existence a meaning—devotion to individuals, groups, or causes; to social, political, intellectual, or creative work. . . . But these possibilities are granted only to a handful of privileged people. It is in the last years of life that the gap between them and the vast majority of mankind becomes deepest and most obvious." [3]

Agreement comes from Arthur Waldman, consultant at the Philadelphia Geriatric Center, who maintains that "senility appears to come more often to the lower end of the intellectual ladder than the top." [4]

But let us not think that a satisfying old age depends on I.Q. or Ph.D. The ladder—intellectual and spiritual— is there to be climbed. It is far too tall to be climbed beginning with the final years of life, however; the climb must start in youth or early adulthood. This truth was well expressed by Bessie Marlin Mason in the simple, honest poem that follows, "Hiram Hill."

He never gazed upon autumn leaves,
  He never sniffed the spring,
He never stopped in the midst of a row
  To hear a bluebird sing.

"You can't eat beauty," Hiram said;
  "You've got to face the facts.
Find me a note in a robin's song
  That'll help me pay my tax!"

"Pigs won't fatten on rainbow sprouts,
  Nor pansy petals, neither.
Watching the clouds won't bring on rain,
  And counting the stars won't, either."

He was always too busy for friendly chat
  With his fellows across the fence;
If somebody's cow got bloated on corn,
  That wasn't Hiram's expense.

He never did warm to the schoolboys' smiles
  As they passed along the lane.
His heart never thrilled with his neighbor's joy,
  Nor throbbed with his neighbor's pain.

Hiram was busy possessing the earth
  And joining field to field.
The only pleasure he ever had
  Was watching his acres yield.

And Hiram grew old possessing the earth,
  And when he was seventy-seven,
He decided to go to the meetinghouse
  And invest in the kingdom of heaven.

Hiram wasn't a wicked man,
   He had never had time to sin,
But he found that his soul was too small to squeeze
   The kingdom of heaven in.[5]

Jesus would have understood Hiram. "Provide your-
selves . . .", he told his followers, "with a treasure in the
heavens that does not fail, where no thief approaches and
no moth destroys" (Luke 12:33). And to the rich young
man genuinely concerned about the good life but tied to
his wealth, Jesus advised, "Sell what you possess and give
to the poor, and you will have treasure in heaven. . . ."
(Matt. 19:21).

"Treasure in heaven" is not a bond issued by a kingdom
beyond the skies. It is a here-and-now spiritual resource
that determines the everlasting quality of human life.
What precisely are the "treasures in heaven" that enrich
and fulfill life from cradle to grave? Toward what "treasures in heaven" may human beings aspire?

A sense of duty done is surely one of the most valuable
treasures a man or woman can collect. On the cross Jesus
made a brief, moving statement of mission accomplished:
"It is finished," he said. And Paul wrote these valedictory
words to Timothy, a young colleague in the Christian
ministry: "The time of my departure has come. I have
fought the good fight. I have finished the race. I have kept
the faith" (2 Tim. 4:6-7).

As age comes on, a sense of duty accomplished, work
completed, brings peace of mind that is truly a heavenly
treasure. The mother muses: "I raised a good family."
The teacher reflects: "I instructed a generation of boys
and girls in knowledge and character." The businessman
balances his life: "I conducted a business that served
real needs of people and was honest in the sight of God."

Has anyone ever expressed more beautifully than John

Henry Cardinal Newman the deep sense of satisfaction a man or woman can experience as the completion of life's mission is contemplated? "O Lord, support us all the day long, until the shadows lengthen and the evening comes, and the busy world is hushed, and the fever of life is over, and our work is done. Then in thy mercy grant us a safe lodging, and a holy rest, and peace at the last. Amen."

A feeling of comradeship with the human family is also a "treasure in heaven." Shakespeare wrote that "crabbed age and youth cannot live together," but age does not have to be crabbed and usually is not. "Grandchildren are God's compensations for growing old," someone said, expressing a universal attitude. Children, like pets, respond to love and attention; age is not a factor in their friendships.

A real problem of adjustment for people of advancing years is the increasing rate of departure of lifetime companions—"four in the last three months," a man of seventy-six lamented. Samuel Johnson made the obvious response: "If a man does not make new acquaintances as he advances through life, he will soon find himself left alone. A man, sir, should keep his friendship in constant repair."[6]

A small-city man, a bachelor devoted to opera, symphony, and theater, decided to move to New York following his retirement. He thought it would be a heaven on earth to live where the best in cultural life could be experienced at will. In a few months he was back home to stay. "Try to imagine what it's like never to have anyone speak to you on the street, never to have a phone call, never to have anyone wonder where or how you are."

Francis J. Braceland, M.D., past president of the American Psychiatric Association, has professional advice of special value to people of increasing age:

Although people usually seem to be the cause of our troubles, the situation would be infinitely worse without

them. Even though patients and parishioners often visual-
ize a lonely retreat and say: "I wish I could get away
from it all and go to a deserted island," our advice should
be, "Don't go." The presence of other human beings is
vital to our existence from birth onward.[7]

Annoying as many people are, association with all kinds
of people is necessary to retain our membership in the
family of man. "Surely there is not a righteous man on
earth . . ." (Eccles. 7:20) is a conclusion all of us are
inclined to agree with at times; but the moral is not to
resign from the human race.

In nursing homes where custodial care is provided,
private rooms are seldom available—and for good reason.
Whether the roommate is considerate and quiet or
demanding and noisy, the therapy is that he or she is
there, unconsciously helping prevent the partner's painful
descent into introspection and self-pity.

The psychologist William James was perceptive when
he wrote: "No more fiendish punishment could be devised,
were such a thing physically possible, than that one should
be turned loose in society and remain absolutely unnoticed
by all the members thereof." Regardless of age, a person
must keep open his channels of communication with living,
reacting human beings. Happiness, longevity depend on it.

Comradeship with the animal world is a cherished
treasure for many people as they move through life. A
boy and his dog are inseparable, but equally dependent
for companionship are elderly people and their dogs, cats,
birds—treasured friends. Despite the growing cost of maintaining pets, owners think of their animal friends as invest-
ments in companionship and peace of mind, not as luxuries.

Such a person was Ella Stifel, a gracious lady—yes,
"lady"—who in her eighties selected this poem by Margaret
Murray to express her love at Christmas-time.

God bless the little things
　　this Christmastide
All the little wild things
　　that live outside
Little cold robins and rabbits
　　in the snow.

Give them good faring and
　　a warm place to go
All the young things
　　for His sake Who died
Who was a little Thing
　　at Christmastide.[8]

Another such inspiring individual was my college organ teacher, Kathryn Beltzhoover Hess, who wrote me years later that "The sunset years have a real glow." She explained, "I have quite a bird-feeding program and am highly entertained by the numerous visits of my many and varied feathered friends. I have a covey of quail which has come with, at times, alarming regularity. Keeping them in feed takes on the proportions of feeding Congress!"

Spontaneous response to the beauties of nature is another rewarding treasure in heaven, as my organ teacher-friend demonstrates. Her letter continues: "I have been living in a winter wonderland the past few days. I took a walk in the stadium woods to enjoy the trees all covered with snow. Then at night I revel in the beauty of the stars on a clear night. Have you noticed Venus in the western sky in the early evening? It is magnificent."

I am reminded of Sir Francis Younghusband's comment, "Clearly it is not the eye but the soul that sees." In the lines that follow, Margaret Farrand tells about ten men who went along a road that offered a view of surpassing beauty.

And all but one passed by,
He saw the hill and the tree and the cloud
With an artist's mind and eye;
He put them down on canvas—
For the other nine men to buy.[9]

Beauty, we are often told, is in the eye of the beholder.
How fortunate, then, is the man or woman of any age
—but especially the person of advanced years whose
travels and experiences are newly limited—when he or
she can find beauty, inspiration, joy, life, in the flower
at the door, the cloud above, "the flash of lovely lifted
wings." Anna Townsend Willis explains to a "dear child,
so young":

Since I've grown old I need to spend
my waking hours on things to tend:
a yellow rose beside my door,
a drift of bright rugs for the floor,
a brown bird's nest in flowering tree—
And you, so young, must pity me
for living in a world so bound
by petty facts of sight and sound.

Dear child, so young, you only see
What time and life have made of me.
You do not know that God is kind,
when we leave youth and strength behind,
to give us joy in little things:
the flash of lovely lifted wings,
the sheets of silvered summer rain,
and fire glow on window pane.

Dear child, I bless each little thing
God gives me for remembering—[10]

Year after year a great-aunt of mine lingered on while friends of the four-score-and-ten-year-old woman thought she would soon move on to the next world. She explained: "I can't imagine not seeing tomorrow morning's newspaper. I want to know how things turn out."

It is this sort of hold on life, this having-something-to-get-up-for-in-the-morning, this tenacious involvement in the world in which we live that keeps people going. "*Always be planning something*," advised a wise old acquaintance of mine. As the later years move on, the scale of our plans is gradually reduced; but if all planning and anticipating stop, in a real sense life stops.

"We prescribe hobbies for the old," Harry Overstreet wrote. "It is as if, in the aging years, all significance drained out of life and only a twiddling of the thumbs remained."[11] Alas, twiddling *is* sometimes the last, last stage of life. If it comes through early senility induced by mental and physical laziness, death before death has indeed arrived and the condition is tragic.

But this is not likely to happen to people who in the days of youth and middle age develop *a lively and growing interest in this exciting universe*: literature, current events, art, music, business, science, photography, sports, travel, theater, politics, space, history, invention, religion, nature, people, radio, TV, etc.

"It is a man's own fault," Samuel Johnson affirmed, "it is from want of use, if his mind grows torpid in old age." [12] Recently I learned of a woman in her ninety-fourth year, confined to a wheelchair because of a broken hip, who reads a book a week, never misses two daily newspapers and a weekly news magazine, and who "never gets tired of seeing people," as her daughter says. She is the kind of person who will *live* until she dies.

Attention in the world of higher education has been drawn to Hastings College of the Law of the University of

California, in San Francisco, where the scandal and waste of "statutory senility," to borrow Dean David Snodgrass's apt term, was successfully challenged. Assembling a distinguished faculty of outstanding law school deans and professors who had been retired at sixty-five by other institutions, the late Dean Snodgrass and his successors have been confident their "65 Club" is a faculty of rare brilliance and vigor.[13] I do not question their evaluation.

Thomas Hart Benton, painter of and for the American people, famous for his mural in the Harry S. Truman Library, Independence, Missouri, and for many other popular works, announced in 1961 that he would paint no more murals. He was seventy-two. He suffered from bursitis. Mural painting, he said, was "just too tough on an old man."

Then he had a stroke. Later he had two heart attacks.

But on March 24, 1973, at the age of eighty-four, Thomas Hart Benton unveiled one of the best murals of his long career, *Joplin at the Turn of the Century.* According to his wife, Rita, as reported by Harris Edward Dark, "While he was hard at his labors, the years seemed to fall from him. He joked with his characters as he painted them, and his famous wit and good humor returned as he seemed to forget he was ever a heart patient. He completed the job in only six months—much sooner than anyone expected."[14]

A deep sense of appreciation for life is clearly one of the most highly valued treasures in heaven. There comes a time when everyone realizes that the years ahead will be few compared with the years behind. But when thankfulness for life and the habit of happiness are in command, there is no despair, no complaining, no fear.

It was in this spirit that Chauncey Depew wrote to his friend Otis Skinner when he learned of Mrs. Skinner's death: "Dear Otis, You lucky bum! Forty blissful years together, you and that enchanting woman."

How different was the graduation speech of David M.
Levy, Dartmouth's highest-ranking graduate a few years
ago. He said to the commencement audience, "I have made
no plans because I have found no plans worth making. . . .
[If you agree with me] tell me how you came to appreciate
the absurdity of your life." [15]

Life is not absurd except for those who think it so.
"A yea-saying to life," says Dr. Eric Pfeiffer, Duke University researcher in geriatrics, contributes mightily to
long life.[16]

We shall not further postpone specific recognition of
these familiar facts: Death is the culmination of old age;
death for some is preceded by poverty, loneliness, disappointment, illness, suffering.

No more realistic description of this kind of old age has
ever been written than is found in the twelfth chapter of
Ecclesiastes (v. 1-2): "Remember also your Creator in the
days of your youth, before the evil days come, and the years
draw nigh, when you will say, 'I have no pleasure in them';
before the sun and the light and the moon and the stars
are darkened and the clouds return after the rain."

What a world of meaning there is in that short clause:
". . . the clouds return after the rain." After rain we want
sunshine and clear skies, not clouds indicating yet more
rain. But age is sometimes marked by recurring misfortune, more clouds, more rain. *Another* trip to the hospital.
Another lifelong friend carried to the grave. *Another* indi-
cation of decreasing vigor. *Another* bout with pain. *Another* day of boredom.

All this *may* happen in the final stage of life; *some* of it
is bound to happen. It is not a pretty prospect. An aging
English professor asked on an examination: "Who wrote
'Grow old along with me! The best is yet to be. . . .'? Name
two other famous liars."

But if "clouds after rain" were a complete description of

typical old age there would be few old people; at seventy-five, eighty, eighty-five they would simply take their lives to avoid what they fear. Though suicide *is* more frequent in old age than during the earlier years, it is by no means so common as to suggest a cop-out practice.

Faith, courage, endurance, health, and ability to adapt to changing conditions are required to reach old age. These qualities and attributes enable most elderly people to live life abundantly to its natural end. Moreover, in the wisdom of age we remember the problems of youth and middle age and know finally that, though difficulties change in the course of life, man is "born to trouble as the sparks fly upward"—just that surely.

There are three periods in the third stage of life: early old age, middle old age, and old old age. Life may end in any of these stages, of course, just as it may end in youth or in middle age. But *life*, not death, is our main consideration, and for most people there is a lot of life in old age, especially if we accept the arbitrary designation of seventy as the start of early old age.

Considering the entire American age group from sixty-five to one hundred, about 85 percent "enjoy comparatively good health," according to Eone Goodenough Hargar, chairman of the Social Research Section of the Gerontological Society. Only 4 to 5 percent live in institutions of any kind, she says—a consoling fact to ponder when visiting a nursing home. An additional 11 percent have disabilities—remember the wide age span in these statistics—that entitle them to the term "shut-in." [17]

The human necessity and obligation, it seems to me, is to accept life in age as in youth. This means to accept life in the spirit of the song writer, Mana-Zucca, whose most popular opus was attempted by every soprano in the days of my youth.

> I love life,
> So I want to live
> And drink of life's fullness,
> Take all it can give.[18]

On his *ninetieth* birthday Justice Oliver Wendell Holmes, Jr., spoke these famous words: ". . . to live is to function. That is all there is to living. And so I close with a line from a Latin poet who uttered the message more than fifteen hundred years ago, 'Death plucks my ear and says: Live—I am coming.'"

On his *ninety-fifth* birthday Sir William Mulock, chief justice of Ontario, told his friends and admirers: "I am still at work, with my hand to the plow, and my face to the future. The shadows of evening lengthen about me, but morning is in my heart. . . . The rich spoils of memory are mine. Mine, too, are the precious things of today—books, flowers, pictures, nature, and sport. The first of May is still an enchanted day to me."

Cicero faced the final stage of old age with serenity: ". . . it is violence that takes life from young men, ripeness from old. This ripeness is so delightful to me that as I approach nearer to death, I seem, as it were, to be coming to port after a long voyage."

Old age does test, and it does reward. The paradox of happiness in old age is that as life nears completion the blend of thankfulness for life and the pain of separation from earth become one doxology to God the Giver. "Swift to its close ebbs out life's little day" is not a cry of complaint but a psalm of praise. With all its heartache, struggle, and pain, life has brought love and beauty and blessing. We are more than content to have lived. We would not have missed life for anything.

But did we succeed? Will we pass the final examination?

In the spirit of Jesus' parable of the sheep and the goats, Ralph Waldo Emerson set forth in memorable language the meaning of success in life. As an epilogue to this chapter on old age, here it is:

> To laugh often and much; to win the respect of intelligent people and the affection of children; to earn the appreciation of honest critics and endure the betrayal of false friends; to appreciate beauty; to find the best in others; to leave the world a bit better, whether by a healthy child, a garden patch, or a redeemed social condition; to know even one life has breathed easier because you lived. This is to have succeeded.

19

DEATH NEED
NOT BE FEARED

Since every person knows from the dawn of consciousness that death is part of the pattern of life, why should anyone fear life's final stage? Yet fear of death is one of the most persistent fears of adults.

Why? Not to *desire* death is one thing, but to *fear* it is something entirely different. Why should anyone be afraid to die?

Part of the explanation lies in fear of the new and unknown. But the experience of those who have met death indicates that, as the end approaches, fear is seldom shown.

Perhaps some fear death because they fear the physical pain of dying. But physicians say that most people endure much more pain during the years when death seems remote than they do in the act of dying.

Fear of separation from loved ones is understandable, but this is love, not fear—a final tribute to life.

Fear of punishment after death may be a real fear for some people, but in most such cases a gnawing sense of regret is the real hell.

What if you, the reader, were told, on the basis of unfavorable medical data, that you should not count on more than one more year of life? How would you react? What would you do?

Most of us have had occasion to consider such situations. A trusted colleague came to my office one unforgettable day to tell me that his doctor had given him just that prediction. My only brother was given three months.

It might be a good idea for all adults, without becoming preoccupied with thoughts of death, to ponder what they would do if they ever had to face a similar situation. I have searched my thoughts on this matter that I might apply my heart unto wisdom. This is what I would do if told I had one year to live.

I would not believe it. At least I would not accept it as final. I would fight for life.

General Eisenhower called himself "a born optimist. I suppose," he said, "most soldiers are, because no soldier ever won a battle if he went into it pessimistically."

Every physician can tell of patients whose lack of hope hastened their death. "It was intrepid of St. Paul," Dr. Karl Menninger remarked, "to declare that hope should stand along with love" in the famous trilogy of faith, hope, and love.

There is considerable evidence that fixing the date of death in one's mind may very well be the cause of death. "In primitive societies the witch doctor was so highly regarded that he could put a curse on a man by saying that he would die on a certain day at six P.M. with the assurance that the victim would almost certainly comply," reports an anthropologist.

Dr. John C. Harvey, professor at Johns Hopkins University Medical School, told his students that "a patient's state of mind can be translated by the body into physiological disorders."

As an illustration, Dr. Harvey told of a woman who en-

tered Baltimore City Hospital three days before her twenty-
third birthday with the conviction that she would die before the birthday arrived. She had been born on a Friday
the thirteenth, she said, and had been hexed by the mid-
wife who attended her birth. The curse was that she would
not live to see her twenty-third birthday.

She died on schedule, of "primary pulmonary hyperten-
sion," and the doctors agree that terror, if not actually the
cause of death, may very well have hastened it.[1]

On the other hand, experienced physicians can tell of
case after case in which a powerful will to live was the
decisive factor in recovery. An American military hospital
treated a patient who became known as "The Man Who
Wouldn't Die." A bullet had entered his right side, passed
through a lung, the diaphragm, gall bladder, and liver.
There were thirteen perforations in his intestines, six of
them double punctures.

"I'll be all right, Doc, don't worry about me," he said
over and over again in the days and weeks during which
his life hung in the balance. Miraculously, it seemed, he
recovered. One of his surgeons commented: "Medical
science is not the last word in saving lives. Any Army doctor knows that. In numerous cases where medical and
surgical skill has failed utterly, the wounded man has recovered by sheer will power."[2]

*Yes, if told I might have only one year to live, I would
fight to live—I would continue to hope. But I would not
ignore the possibility that the prediction might come true.
What would I do besides fighting for life—and hoping?*

I would accustom myself to a fact that I had known all
along but only half realized—that for me as for everyone
else death is inevitable.

It is likely that no man or woman can face this truth
realistically until death steps out of the shadows and
beckons. But the moment comes—a heart attack, a cancer

diagnosis, a terrible wreck, a birthday late in life, a soldier's order to enter the combat area.

This realization implies coming to terms with God. It means acceptance, once and for all remaining time, of death as part of life, as natural and as friendly as birth.

Montaigne, the French essayist, conveyed this assurance in words of exceeding simplicity: "Death is not to be feared. It is a friend. The time you leave behind was no more yours than that which was before your birth and concerns you no more. Make room for others as others have done for you. . . . Depart without fear out of this world even as you came into it. Yield your torch to others as in a race. Your death is but a piece of the world's order, a parcel of the world's life." [3]

With this approach to the final level of human experience we can better understand the epitaph Robert Louis Stevenson wrote for his Samoan grave:

> Under the wide and starry sky,
> Dig the grave and let me lie:
> Glad did I live and gladly die,
> And I laid me down with a will. [4]

We are certain that at forty-four Stevenson did not want to die. Indeed his dogged fight for life against the ravages of tuberculosis, in days when relatively little was known about fighting the disease, is striking evidence of his will to live.

But Stevenson, having taken his stand and fought his battle, died as he lived, gladly and willingly. He had come to terms with God and the life he had given. The habit of happiness sustained him to the end.

Having accepted the possibility that the medical estimate might be correct, and having made certain that I was prepared spiritually both to live and to die, I would then make sure that my business was in order.

This would be a simple undertaking. Insurance settlement provisions would be checked. The will would be looked over and revised if necessary. Social Security records would be investigated. Any debts would be cleared up if possible. Everything would be done that would ease the way for those who would be left—especially one.

And then, so far as humanly possible, I would go on living as if nothing had happened.

This is exactly what William Rainey Harper, first president of the University of Chicago, did when he learned that malignancy was involved in the appendectomy that at first seemed routine. He wrote to his friend, F. T. Gates: "The operation will take place within two weeks. I have often wondered how a man felt when notified that within fourteen or sixteen days he might have to close up his account. I shall not have the occasion to wonder much longer."

Four days later Dr. Harper reported to his friend: "I have met my classes today as usual and have lectured to the freshmen. . . . I find that I am very much better off working than doing nothing." [5]

I do not know who wrote the poem found in the papers of my wife's father, a minister who to the end of his long life lived every line of the following:

> Let me die working,
> Still tackling plans unfinished, tasks undone.
> Clean to its end, swift may my race be run,
> No lagging steps, no faltering, no shirking:
> Let me die working.
>
> Let me die thinking,
> Let me fare forth still with an open mind,

Fresh secrets to unfold, new truths to find,
My soul undimmed, alert, no question blinking:
Let me die thinking.

Let me die giving,
The substance of life for life's enriching.
Time, things and self to heaven converging,
No selfish thought—loving, redeeming, living:
Let me die giving.

The way to prepare to die is to prepare to live—to do the things we ought to do, and eventually to die with as few regrets as humanly possible.

It is the fear of death with unsettled accounts in the book of life that produces fears at the end, and properly so. The person who has savagely pushed his way through life with little thought for the hurts and injuries he has inflicted on others, with concern only for his own pleasure and profit, has no "treasures in heaven"—no sense of mission accomplished, no assurance of peace with man and God, no feeling that it matters whether he lived or not. This, truly, is hell, and it may be endless.

"If thou art not in heaven in this life," said Charles Kingsley, "thou wilt never be in heaven in the life to come." This is enough to know about life after death. To prepare is the duty of man; the rest is up to God. The purpose of religion, as I see it, is not to get people into a future heaven; it is to get the heavenly quality of life into people here and now.

If modern man could get rid of the notion that the future life is continued *physical* existence in a *physical* environment, most doubt and confusion in this area would be eliminated. A physical concept of immortality has never been Christian doctrine, but the same kind of mind that has difficulty translating Santa Claus into Spirit of Love has always had trouble comprehending the plain New Testament teaching on this subject.

Harry Emerson Fosdick said that during his seminary days he came to his professor of theology, William Newton Clarke, with this sincere problem: "I just can't see how Jesus can be physically divine." The grand old theologian looked his student straight in the eye and replied with a self-answering counter question: *"Physically* divine?"

This impossible paradox is no more impossible than the vague impression that a photograph of a man taken the day before his death and a photograph taken by the same kind of camera a thousand years later "in eternity" would produce the same print—or possibly even the image of the man fifty years before his death.

To be sure, certain interpreters of Christianity have contributed to the confusion. "Resurrection of the *body*" in the Apostles' Creed has been generally left unexplained even in terms of "resurrection body," "spiritual body," or to quote St. Paul again, "immortality." The veneration of human bones thought to have been part of the anatomy of certain long-deceased saints has sometimes been explained in terms of their future reassembly "in heaven."

Fortunately, such confusion is diminishing, but the result is too often the kind of false-front bravery implied by the observation, "When you're dead, you're dead." For *this*, surely, has never been Christian doctrine. Basic is the unifying concept of a deathless Spirit who created us, from whom we came, and to whom eventually we return in the Spirit of Christ.

Some of the very first Christians, it appears, found it difficult to accept a spiritual afterlife as significant or satisfying. St. Paul devoted a major section of his first letter to the church at Corinth to the obvious truth, which was apparently not fully understood or accepted. "It is sown a physical body, it is raised a spiritual body. . . . I tell you this, brethren: flesh and blood cannot inherit the kingdom of God, nor does the perishable inherit the imperishable, and this mortal nature must put on immortality." (1 Cor. 15:44, 50, 53).

Contrary to the embroidery occasionally added to basic New Testament statements, Jesus provided no blueprint for the future life. But he believed and he demonstrated that life is continuous.

Regardless of how a modern follower of Jesus "pictures" the Easter event, he does not question it. His own experience will not let him doubt that Jesus lives to this very day. But Jesus did not describe to his disciples precisely what form the "everlasting life" takes after the "earthly house" is dissolved.

We can be certain, nevertheless, that a human life does not end when the heart stops beating. A momentum of soul lives on as a personal contribution to the continuing life of humanity. Though the tributary stream has joined the mainstream of ongoing mankind, the individual soul— whether developed in the direction of truth, beauty, goodness, or the opposite—continues to affect the nature of that stream forever.

Thus men live after death not only in their books, their music, their pictures, their buildings, their influence, their children and grandchildren, but in the very soul of humankind, the heart of God. Not a particle of spirit is lost. This is the assurance Jesus sought to convey to his disciples.

The Christian believes that God has charged individual man with responsibility for purifying and renewing the stream of human life. He recognizes and accepts the cycle of individual birth and death as God's principal means for achieving this end.

This is what Paul meant when he declared, "Death is swallowed up in victory" (1 Cor. 15:54). For death, which is known and expected from the beginning of life, is not defeat. Death is truthfully "swallowed up in victory" because death is the triumph of life, the completion of the task, the accomplishment of the mission.

When, on the cross, Jesus said, "It is finished" (John 19:30), his was no cry of failure or frustration but rather an exultant declaration of success. Some scholars believe the Aramaic expression Jesus used for "It is finished" was the same as that used in his time by a victorious runner in a race. It means "I have won!" [6]

Paul expressed himself in very similar language when he faced the untimely end of his Christian ministry: "I have fought the good fight, I have finished the race, I have kept the faith" (2 Tim. 4:7).

"The great use of a life," said William James in like vein, "is to spend it for something that outlasts it."

The cynic who believes that man is predestined to defeat because from the beginning he knows he must die is a person to be pitied. Such a person is fighting the universe. He denies God and condemns himself to a lifetime of unhappy refusal to accept the everlasting life.

Quality, not *quantity*, distinguishes everlasting life. When Emerson was only twenty-nine years of age he wrote, "Don't tell me to get ready to die. I know not what shall be. The only preparation I can make is by fulfilling my present duties. This is the everlasting life." St. John agreed: ". . . whoever believes in him should not perish but have eternal life"—NOW.

Man creates his hell or his heaven by the choices he makes. What he has chosen he *is* and *will be* down through eons while soul echoes to soul through endless corridors of timeless existence.

This may help us to understand the confidence with which Emerson wrote in his diary: "I do not fear death. . . . I should lie down in the lap of earth as trustingly as ever on my own bed." [7]

20

HAPPINESS COMES
UNINVITED (A Summation)

The notion that happiness can or should be pursued is fixed in the consciousness of Americans probably because the Declaration of Independence lists "the pursuit of happiness" with life and liberty as primary rights of all human beings.

Thomas Jefferson, however, was likely thinking more of the political approach to individual happiness than the philosophical or religious. Governments, he believed, should not limit a citizen's choice of thought or life-style, unless the citizen's choice should interfere with the parallel right of another citizen.

Happiness in a profound sense, of course, has little relationship to the ups and downs of the passing days. We all know that some days will be loaded with pleasant experiences, that others will bring mostly the opposite.

If we pursue any goal in life, then, it is not a kind of life in which we are gloriously, deliriously happy every minute of the day and night. The happiness of good news, blue skies, delicious meals, friendly people, perfect health, a full bank account, unquestioned love is not a state anyone is destined to enjoy forever.

The paradox of happiness is the truth that in the midst of unhappiness man can find happiness. The alternative to accepting this paradox is not a philosophy of realism, agnosticism, atheism, or the ancient goal of imperturbability. The real alternative is hopelessness, despair, defeat, isolation, spiritual suicide.

Is there a better term than "happiness" for the quality of life desired by all men and women? Joshua Loth Liebman, the young rabbi who produced a best-selling book titled *Peace of Mind*, was certain he had found one. Broadly understood, "peace of mind" does indeed describe the happiness of one who has achieved a basic victory over selfishness, self-pity, hatred, and uselessness.

The over-tranquilized zombie who has been given a medical retreat from the arena of life can scarcely be said to have peace of mind. Unless he is able to resume control of his life, he will no more have peace of mind than a drunken New Year's Eve celebrant, singing "I Want to Be Happy," will have abiding happiness.

"Contentment," if not narrowly applied, is a good term for a human life in happy balance between Utopia and reality. St. Paul, whose years as a Christian were seldom easy, wrote to his friends at Philippi, "I have learned, in whatever state I am, to be content" (Phil. 4:11).

A twelve-year-old girl wrote:

> It is a gray day.
> And I am happy.
> I am not happy because something special is
> going to happen,
> I am happy because I am content. . . .[1]

But "happiness," "peace of mind," "contentment" are not synonymous with "complacency" or "resignation."

J. S. Mill had the right idea when he wrote, "It is better

to be a human being dissatisfied than a pig satisfied; better to be Socrates dissatisfied than a fool satisfied." [2] Contentment on the human level reflects a state of balance between ambition and accomplishment, between one's ideals and one's mode of life. This, obviously, is not the description of a contented cow.

It is *tension,* welcomed and directed, that ultimately produces contentment, peace of mind, happiness. Without the normal tension that makes us human, we are powerless on the road of life. Movement from what we are to what we want to be comes from healthy tension, as normal and necessary as the tension in the mainspring of a watch.

People in the middle of life, crowded with the demands of children, job, security, sometimes complain of life's tensions. If they complain too much, if they feel too sorry for themselves, *unhealthy* tension may develop and have serious consequences. Later in life these people will likely look back to the busiest, most hectic years of their experience as the happiest years of their lives.

In July 1940, Winston Churchill, prime minister of Great Britain, vetoed a Navy request that the Mediterranean fleet move to Gibraltar to avoid air attack. His brusque refusal ended with these words, "Warships are meant to go under fire." [3]

And so are people! "Let us seek respite where it is—in the thick of battle," advised Albert Camus. The legendary Paganini, violin virtuoso, so a story goes, provoked laughter when he limped to the stage because of a nail in his shoe, knocked over a candle while tuning his instrument, and suffered a broken string as soon as he began to play. The laughter became hysterical when a second and then a third string snapped. But Paganini did not stop. From one string he elicited sounds so sublime, so unbelievable that the audience was reduced to awed silence.

When nineteen-year-old Jill Kinmont, one of our country's finest skiers, crashed in a pre-Olympic race, she
became a quadriplegic, unable to move or feel anything
below her shoulders. Later she described her first reaction,
"I started thinking what you can do with what you have."
Jill completed college. She became a teacher.[4]

Happiness is not the absence of misfortune. Happiness
is the ability to handle misfortune. It involves the oft-
noted ability to cooperate with the inevitable.

When the sick encountered Jesus, they were not given
sermons on the problem of evil. Jesus recognized the dark
side of life as part of the nature of the universe. The
reality of evil, illness, suffering, and death, he believed,
was neither to be accepted nor rejected; man has no such
choice. But he can recognize the totality of life and, with
God's step-by-step guidance, he can develop a positive
faith strong enough to support life.

Through the gloom of the Last Supper with Jesus'
disciples came the exultant word "joy." "These things I
have spoken to you," he said, "that my joy may be in you,
and that your joy may be full" (John 15:11). If the
disciples failed to find joy in talk of betrayal and death,
they were nevertheless challenged to discover joy in doing
God's will.

"In the world you have tribulation," Jesus agreed, "but
be of good cheer, I have overcome the world. . . . In me
you may have peace" (John 16:33). To overcome is to
find peace.

This, clearly, is the opposite of the notion that happiness
is something you chase. The pursuit of happiness is not
a Saturday-night–special of booze and broads. Entertain-
ment, pleasure, fun come on different levels for different
types of people on different occasions, but the funda-
mental factors of a happy life are qualities of the spirit.

"Happiness in this world, when it comes," wrote Nathaniel Hawthorne, "comes incidentally. Make it the object of pursuit, and it leads us on a wild-goose chase, and is never attained. Follow some other object, and very possibly we may find that we have caught happiness without dreaming of it. . . ."

The truly happy people are those who genuinely love one or more human beings, who have responsibilities—big or little—that give them a sense of being needed, and who are dedicated to a worthwhile cause with which they are happy to be associated.

Happiness, then, is only remotely associated with wealth or fame or good times. Happy people may have one or all of these supposed blessings, of course, but happiness is likely to have existed first. "He who loves money," wrote the author of Ecclesiastes, "will not be satisfied with money" (Eccles. 5:10). If happiness really depended upon *getting* something, few people could be happy often or for long.

The kingdom of happiness is within. *Being* rather than getting is the key. Happiness comes uninvited. It is pursued unwittingly, unconsciously.

Ignazio Silone would agree. In *Bread and Wine* he wrote, "A silly life is based on appearances. It aims only at seeming. . . . To the stupid, being is not important, seeming is." [5]

Lasting happiness comes from what we really are, from *being* something.

But only the wise know this.

NOTES

Selections from the Bible are (except as noted) from the Revised Standard Version copyrighted (Old Testament 1952, New Testament 1971) by the Division of Christian Education of the National Council of the Churches of Christ in the United States of America.

CHAPTER 1

1. Ludwig van Beethoven, letter to Franz Wegeler, November 16, 1800 or 1801.
2. Chauncey D. Leake, *What Are We Living For? Practical Philosophy: The Ethics* (Westbury: PJD Publications Ltd., 1973), p. 107.
3. Thomas Curtis Clark, "When I Am Old," from *Poems for Life* (Chicago: Willett, Clark, 1941), p. 32. Copyright © 1941 by Thomas Curtis Clark. Reprinted by permission of Harper & Row, Publishers, Inc. (p. 7)

CHAPTER 2

1. Ella Wheeler Wilcox, from "Beyond." By permission of Rand McNally Co., successors to W. B. Conkey Co., Chicago.
2. John Ruskin, *The Crown of Wild Olive*, in *The Works of John Ruskin*, edited by E. T. Cook and Alexander Wedderburn (New York: Longmans, Green, & Co., 1903–1912), XVIII, 497.
3. Excerpt from Act III ("I can't. I can't go on . . . . every, every minute?") in *Our Town* by Thornton Wilder. Copyright 1938, 1957 by Thornton Wilder. Reprinted by permission of Harper & Row, Publishers, Inc., and by permission of Penguin Books, publishers of the British edition. (p. 13)
4. Cortlandt W. Sayres, "Bankrupt," in *Poems That Live Forever*, compiled by Hazel Fellemann (Garden City, N.Y.: Doubleday & Co., 1965), p. 295. Copyright Christian Century Foundation. Reprinted by permission from *The Christian Century*.

CHAPTER 3

1. Carol Ruth Sternhell, "The Good Life on Earth," *McCall's*, 97:36 (January 1970).
2. William Wordsworth, *Lines Composed a Few Miles above Tintern Abbey*.
3. Mary Littledale, "Winter Wood," *Poetry*, February 1937. Copyright 1948 by the Modern Poetry Association and reprinted by permission of the editor of *Poetry*.
4. Wendell White, *Psychology in Living* (New York: Macmillan Co., 1947). Condensation of a chapter reprinted in *Journal of Living*, January 1948, p. 17.
5. Anne Frank, *The Diary of a Young Girl* (New York: Doubleday & Co., 1952), p. 278.
6. Folliott S. Pierpoint, "For the Beauty of the Earth."
7. Robert Burns, "To a Mouse."
8. John Glenn, *Life*, 52:30 (March 9, 1962).
9. Lillian Smith, "Awakening of the Heart," *Redbook*, 119:22 (August 1962).
10. Carl Sandburg, *Remembrance Rock* (New York: Harcourt, Brace & Co., 1948), p. 1,063.

CHAPTER 4

1. Samuel Taylor Coleridge, "Kubla Khan."
2. Edmund Burke, from letter to William Smith, January 9, 1795.
3. Elbert Hubbard, *An American Bible* (New York: Wm. H. Wise & Co., 1946), p. 245.

CHAPTER 5

1. Quoted by Kenneth Clark, *New York Times*, April 12, 1971.
2. *University College Quarterly* (Michigan State), January 1970, p. 16.
3. George R. Stewart, *Man—An Autobiography* (New York: Random House, 1946), p. 291.
4. William Shakespeare, *Hamlet*, II.ii.16–17.
5. Copyright 1947 The Christian Century Foundation. Reprinted by permission from the March 12, 1947, issue of *The Christian Century*, p. 333.
6. Pittsburgh *Post-Gazette*, October 31, 1970.
7. Jean-Francois Revel, *Without Marx or Jesus* (Garden City, N. Y.: Doubleday & Co., 1971), pp. 116–117.

8. Edgar Lee Masters, "Lucinda Matlock," *Spoon River Anthology* (New York: Macmillan Co., 1933), p. 229. Copyright 1944 by Edgar Lee Masters.Printed with permission of the Estate of Edgar Lee Masters.

CHAPTER 6

1. Immanuel Kant, *Critique of Pure Reason* (1791), Conclusion.
2. William Shakespeare, *Hamlet*, I.iii.78–80.
3. "The Wisdom of Albert Schweitzer," *Wisdom Magazine*, February 1956.
4. Elizabeth York Case, "Unbelief," Detroit *Free Press*.
5. Maltbie D. Babcock, *Thoughts for Everyday Living* (New York: Charles Scribner's Sons, 1901).
6. Alfred Tennyson, "In Memoriam A. H. H.," Prologue, Stanza 6.
7. Though not described in theological language, the immanence and the transcendence of God have been affirmed.
8. Copyright 1947 by E. E. Cummings; copyright 1975 by Nancy T. Andrews. Reprinted from *Complete Poems 1913-1962* by E. E. Cummings, by permission of Harcourt Brace Jovanovich, Inc., and by permission of Granada Publishing Limited (U.K.).

CHAPTER 7

1. Samuel M. Shoemaker, *How You Can Find Happiness* (New York: E. P. Dutton & Co., 1947), p. 114.
2. Anne Reeve Aldrich, "A Little Parable," in *An American Anthology 1787–1900*, edited by Edmund Clarence Stedman (Boston: Houghton Mifflin Co., *c.* 1900), p. 720.
3. Annie Johnson Flint, "What God Has Promised." Reprinted by permission of Evangelical Publishers, Toronto, Ontario.

CHAPTER 8

1. Joyce Cary, "Child's Religion," *Vogue*, 122:86–87 (December 1953).
2. "The Wisdom of Albert Schweitzer," *Wisdom Magazine*, February 1956.

CHAPTER 9

1. Alfred Tennyson, "In Memoriam A. H. H.," Section CXVIII, Stanza 7.

2. Erich Fromm, *The Anatomy of Human Destructiveness* (New York: Holt, Rinehart & Winston, 1973), p. 9.
3. Mark Twain, *The Adventures of Huckleberry Finn* (Garden City, N.Y.: American Headquarters, International Collectors Edition, c. 1955), pp. 215–216.
4. John Masefield, *The Trial of Jesus* (London: W. Heinemann, 1925).

CHAPTER 10

1. William Shakespeare, *The Merchant of Venice*, I.i.13–14.
2. Harry Emerson Fosdick, *The Meaning of Being a Christian* (New York: Association Press, 1964), p. 118.
3. Reinhold Niebuhr, "Some Things I Have Learned," *Saturday Review*, 48:63 (November 6, 1965).
4. Harry Emerson Fosdick, *The Living of These Days* (New York: Harper & Brothers, 1956), p. 219.

CHAPTER 12

1. Harry Emerson Fosdick, *Living under Tension* (New York: Harper & Brothers, 1941), p. 162.
2. Harry and Bonaro Overstreet, *The Mind Alive* (New York: W. W. Norton & Co., 1954), chapter 15.

CHAPTER 13

1. Herbert A. Otto, "Has Monogamy Failed?" *Saturday Review*, 53:24 (April 25, 1970).
2. Richard D. Lyons, "Marriage: It's Still Popular in the U. S.," *New York Times*, December 2, 1971.
3. Anne Roiphe, "Marriage," *Vogue*, 165:103 (January 1975).
4. William J. Lederer, "Putting Marriage on Camera," *National Observer*, March 24, 1973, p. 26. Copyright 1973 by the NYM Corporation; printed first in *New York Magazine*.
5. WINS radio, New York.
6. "I Never Knew (I Could Love Anybody Like I'm Loving You)," W/M: Tom Pitts, Ray Egan, Roy K. Marsh. Copyright © 1920, renewed 1947. Used by permission of Leo Feist, Inc., New York.
7. Anne Morrow Lindbergh, *Dearly Beloved* (New York: Harcourt, Brace & World, 1962), p. 171.

8. Georgie Starbuck Galbraith, "Love's Season Is Brief," *McCall's*, 91:226 (October 1963). Used by permission of *McCall's*.

9. John Nef, *A Search for Civilization* (Chicago: Henry Regnery Co., 1962), p. 28.

10. Ashley Montagu, *On Being Human* (New York: Schuman, 1951), p. 80.

11. Quoted in Mary S. Christie's *O Infinite Mystery* (n.p., 1967), p. 58.

CHAPTER 14

1. According to Robert H. Browning, Professor of Medicine, The Ohio State University, as cited in *New York Times*, June 30, 1967.

2. According to Eldon K. Siebel, chest surgeon, Dallas, Texas, UPI, 1963.

3. According to a research study conducted at Roswell Park Memorial Institute, Buffalo, reported in *Journal of the American Dental Association*, 1968.

4. *Consumer Bulletin*, Consumers' Research, Inc., Washington, N. J., July 1958, p. 12.

5. According to the National Center for Health Statistics.

CHAPTER 15

1. Alfred Tennyson, "Break, Break, Break," Stanza 3.

2. Olivia de Havilland, "The Best Advice I Ever Had," *Reader's Digest*, 76:123 (March 1960).

3. Alfred Tennyson, "In Memoriam A. H. H.," Section XXVIII, Stanza 4.

4. Ibid., Section LXXVIII, Stanza 4.

5. Ibid., Section LXXXV, Stanza 15.

6. Quoted by Joshua Loth Liebman, *Peace of Mind* (New York: Simon & Schuster, 1946), p. 122.

7. John A. Schindler, *How To Live 365 Days a Year* (New York: Prentice-Hall, 1954), p. 9.

8. Clarence E. Macartney, "Troubles Are Teachers," *Wisdom Magazine*.

9. Robert Louis Stevenson, *Our Samoan Adventure*, edited by Charles Neider (New York: Harper & Brothers, 1955). Quoted from *New York Times Book Review*, Sept. 18, 1955, p. 10.

10. Quoted by Arthur and Barbara Gelb, "As O'Neill Saw the Theatre," *New York Times Magazine*, November 12, 1961, p. 32.

CHAPTER 16

1. Dana L. Farnsworth and Francis J. Braceland, *Psychiatry, the Clergy and Pastoral Counseling* (Collegeville, Minn.: St. John's University Press, 1969), p. 291.
2. Kenneth Vanderbeek, "A Gross Social Display," *Bethany Tower* (Bethany College, Bethany, W. Va.), February 27, 1975.
3. Farnsworth and Braceland, *op. cit.*, pp. 89–90.
4. From an address given in 1968 when Dr. Silber was Dean of the College of Arts and Sciences, University of Texas.
5. Will and Ariel Durant, *The Lessons of History* (New York: Simon & Schuster, 1968), p. 36.
6. Paul Laurence Dunbar, from "The Debt," *The Complete Poems of Paul Laurence Dunbar* (New York: Dodd, Mead & Co., 1929), p. 213.
7. William Sloane Coffin, Jr. " 'Not Yet a Good Man,' " *New York Times*, June 19, 1973.
8. *Time*, 103:14 (June 3, 1974).
9. *Wall Street Journal*, February 5, 1974.
10. Quoted by Steven M. Spencer, "The Drug Scene: Marijuana," *Reader's Digest*, 96:69 (January 1970).
11. D. Harvey Powelson, M.D., "Marijuana: More Dangerous Than You Know," *Reader's Digest*, 105:95–99 (December 1974).
12. Jane E. Brody, *New York Times*, January 11, 1974.
13. Ibid.
14. Robert Campbell, Director, Department of Psychiatry, St. Vincent's Hospital, *New York Times*, June 25, 1971.
15. "Alcoholism: New Victims, New Treatment," *Time*, 103:75 (April 22, 1974).
16. Joseph A. Bartell, former Dean of Students, West Liberty State College, West Liberty, W. Va. Personal communication.
17. Alex Majewski, Unit Supervisor, Alcoholic Program, South Hills Health System, Pittsburgh, Pa. Personal communication.
18. *Time*, 103:75 (April 22, 1974).
19. *Wall Street Journal*, October 15, 1973.
20. Jane E. Brody, *New York Times*, January 1, 1972.
21. *Wall Street Journal*, October 1, 1973.
22. *Life*, 69:39 (November 20, 1970).
23. Quoted in an Ann Landers column, Wheeling *News-Register*.

24. Rollo May, *Love and Will* (New York: W. W. Norton & Co., 1969), p. 42.

CHAPTER 17

1. Carolyn Wells, "My Boon." Permission granted by Maurice O'Connell.
2. Hervey Allen, *Anthony Adverse* (New York: Farrar & Rinehart, 1933), p. 447.
3. Edna St. Vincent Millay, "Ashes of Life," from *Collected Poems*, Harper & Row. Copyright 1917, 1945 by Edna St. Vincent Millay. Used by permission of Norma Millay Ellis.
4. Frank S. Caprio and Joseph R. Berger, *Helping Yourself with Self-Hypnosis* (Englewood Cliffs, N. J.: Prentice-Hall, 1963), pp. 182–183.
5. Henry David Thoreau, *Journal*, July 14, 1852.
6. Morris Kertzer, "Face to Face with Gabriel," in *Guideposts*.
7. Margaret Bailey, "A Prayer," in *The Treasury of Religious Verse*, compiled by Donald T. Kauffman (Westwood, N. J.: Fleming H. Revell Co., 1962), p. 109.
8. Harry Emerson Fosdick, *Riverside Sermons* (New York: Harper & Brothers, 1958), p. 135.
9. Charles A. Lindbergh, *The Spirit of St. Louis* (New York: Charles Scribner's Sons, 1953), pp. 302–303.
10. *Wall Street Journal*, December 1968.
11. Max Ehrmann, *Desiderata*, 1927.
12. William H. Sheldon, *Psychology and the Promethean Will* (New York: Harper & Brothers, 1936), p. 3.
13. Joshua Loth Liebman, *Peace of Mind* (New York: Simon & Schuster, 1946), p. 101.
14. William Shakespeare, *Hamlet*, III.iv.67–69.
15. C. S. Lewis, *The Screwtape Letters* (New York: Macmillan Co., 1951), p. 143.

CHAPTER 18

1. Anne Bradstreet, "Meditations Divine and Moral," in *The Works of Anne Bradstreet*, edited by Jeannine Hensley (Cambridge: Belknap Press, 1967), p. 272.
2. Sydney Harris, syndicated column, Pittsburgh *Post-Gazette*, November 2, 1974.
3. Simone de Beauvoir, *The Coming of Age*, translated by Patrick O'Brian (New York: G. P. Putnam's Sons, 1972), pp. 540–541.
4. Douglas S. Looney, quoted in *National Observer*, March 31, 1973.

5. Bessie Marlin Mason, "Hiram Hill," *Saturday Evening Post*, 212:70 (May 25, 1940). Reprinted with permission from the *Saturday Evening Post*. © 1940 The Curtis Publishing Company.
6. Quoted in James Boswell, *The Life of Samuel Johnson.* Modern Library edition (New York: Random House, 1952), p. 86.
7. Dana L. Farnsworth and Francis J. Braceland, *Psychiatry, the Clergy and Pastoral Counseling* (Collegeville, Minn.: St. John's University Press, 1969), p. 140.
8. From a greeting card.
9. Margaret Farrand, "The Seeing Eye," in *The Independent.*
10. Anna Townsend Willis, "Rosemary," in *Modern Maturity.* By permission of author and publisher.
11. Harry A. Overstreet, *The Mature Mind* (New York: W. W. Norton & Co., 1949), p. 291.
12. Quoted in James Boswell, *The Life of Samuel Johnson.* Modern Library edition (New York: Random House, 1952), p. 379.
13. *College Management*, 5:28–29 (March 1970).
14. Harris Edward Dark, "Thomas Hart Benton Paints Again," *Modern Maturity*, June-July 1973, p. 34.
15. *New York Times*, June 14, 1971.
16. *Newsweek*, 82:66 (April 16, 1973).
17. Reported in *Oberlin Alumni Magazine*, September-October 1974, p. 16.
18. Mana-Zucca, "I Love Life." Copyright 1923, renewed 1962, John Church Company. Permission granted by Estates of Irwin Cassel and Mana-Zucca.

CHAPTER 19

1. Associated Press dispatch, Pittsburgh *Post-Gazette*, November 17, 1967.
2. Bob Davis, "The Man Who Wouldn't Die," New York *Sun*, condensed and reprinted in *Reader's Digest*, 35:41–42 (October 1939).
3. Michel de Montaigne, adapted from essay (I, 19) "That To Study Philosophy Is To Learn To Die."
4. Robert Louis Stevenson, "Requiem."
5. T. W. Goodspeed, *William Rainey Harper* (Chicago: University of Chicago Press, 1928).
6. Mary S. Christie, *O Infinite Mystery* (n.p. 1967), p. 19.
7. *The Journals and Miscellaneous Notebooks of Ralph Waldo Emerson*, edited by William H. Gilman and Alfred R. Ferguson (Cambridge: Harvard University Press, Belknap Press, 1963), p. 312.

CHAPTER 20

1. Flora J. Arnstein, *Adventure into Poetry* (Stanford: Stanford University Press, 1951), p. 114.
2. John Stuart Mill, *Utilitarianism* (1863). Reprinted in *Great Books of the Western World,* edited by Robert Maynard Hutchins and others (Chicago: Encyclopaedia Britannica, 1952), XLIII, 449.
3. Winston Churchill, *Their Finest Hour,* Vol. II of *The Second World War* (Boston: Houghton Mifflin Co., 1949), p. 443.
4. "What You Can Do with What You Have," *Life* 56:75 (June 19, 1964).
5. Ignazio Silone, *Bread and Wine* (New York and London: Harper & Brothers, 1937), p. 303.